How to Know the Minerals and
Rocks offers 7 keys to the identification of minerals
1. Luster
2. Hardness
3. Color
4. Streak
5. Cleavage
6. Fracture
7. Specific gravity

and 4 keys to the identification
of rocks
1. Texture and structure
2. Color
3. Acid test
4. Mineral content

RICHARD M. PEARL
is Professor of Geology at
Colorado College, and the author
of "Popular Gemology", "Mineral
Collectors Handbook", and other
books.

D0061609

McGRAW-HILL PAPERBACKS
HOBBY AND PROFESSIONAL GUIDES

How to Know
the Minerals and Rocks

Richard M. Pearl

Arthur B. Merkle

McGraw-Hill Book Company, Inc.
New York   Toronto   London

Dedicated
in gratitude and affection to
Lillian Drews Garvin

PUBLISHED BY THE MC GRAW-HILL BOOK COMPANY, INC.
PRINTED IN THE UNITED STATES OF AMERICA

678910 MUMU 7654
ISBN 07-049021-X

Preface

How to Know the Minerals and Rocks is a practical field guide to more than 125 of the most important minerals and rocks, including gems, ores, native metals, meteorites, and other interesting members of the mineral kingdom. It is simplified, authoritative, and up to date—written for the layman and for the beginning and amateur collector. With it you can identify for yourself the better-quality typical specimens you are most likely to find, as well as others of outstanding interest to collectors, prospectors, and scientists.

Even many fairly advanced collectors of minerals are unable to recognize by name the commonest rocks, because of their diverse appearance and the lack of definite tests for them. The Four Keys to Recognizing Rocks make it easy to identify the chief types by a simple but systematic procedure.

Similarly, the Seven Keys to Recognizing Minerals enable the new collector to become acquainted quickly with the important minerals which make up the majority of those he will come across in this fascinating and fast-growing hobby. Moreover, no special skill is needed to make the tests, and no equipment other than a pocket-knife, a common magnet, a piece of broken porcelain, a piece of glass, a copper coin, a piece of quartz, and some vinegar.

Although the author believes wholeheartedly in the value of the standard blowpipe methods for testing minerals and has taught them to many students, they are not employed in this book because of the proved reluctance of most collectors to attempt their use without personal instruction. A few other kinds of tests are mentioned, but the minerals can be identified without them.

Besides the Keys for mineral and rock identification, this book has more unique features. Each description of a mineral or a rock is accompanied by a drawing which brings out clearly the typical appearance and the characteristics by which the mineral or rock can be recognized. These well-labeled drawings, based upon sketches that were made especially for this book by the author's wife and were prepared in close collaboration with his writing of the text, will prove more valuable to the collector than pages of explanation.

The description of certain minerals includes handy tips on collecting, handling, cleaning, preserving, or displaying them—information not readily available elsewhere. The descriptions also cover the chemical composition, occurrence, uses, historical lore, and a range of other entertaining and informative background material on each mineral and rock.

Simplified information is given for learning how to read the chemical formulas of minerals. A list is presented of all the national magazines in the United States devoted to mineral and rock collecting and related hobbies. A selected reading list of books on these subjects is given, with brief descriptions to aid you in purchasing them.

Other distinctive features of this book include careful attention to scientific words so that all such words are explained when first used; emphasis of technical words by italics; thoughtful selection of photographs to tie in with the text and illustrate the discussion; and a complete Index.

Richard M. Pearl

COLORADO SPRINGS, COLO.

Contents

Acknowledgments

In addition to preparing preliminary sketches for almost all the drawings, my wife, Mignon W. Pearl, has given careful attention to the rest of the manuscript, and her advice has been extremely helpful. Eva C. Keller, of Colorado Springs, designed one of the difficult illustrations. Dr. Don B. Gould, of Colorado College, helpfully supplied a needed item of information. Nordis Felland, Librarian of the American Geographical Society, New York, checked some geographic names.

Stephen J. Voorhies prepared the line drawings that appear throughout this book.

I wish to express my gratitude to the following for color illustrations: Henry L. Gresham of Ward's Natural Science Establishment, Rochester, N. Y., who made available the photographs of minerals from the Harvard University Collection; Harry B. Groom, Jr., Assistant Professor of Geology, Louisiana Polytechnic Institute, whose photographs of minerals in the Harvard Collection appear on the jacket; and *Leica Photography Magazine,* in the pages of which Professor Groom's photographs were first reproduced.

R. M. P.

CHAPTER 1

This Fascinating Mineral Hobby

Collectors of minerals and rocks are rapidly becoming more numerous all over the world, especially in the United States and Canada. This has been true for about twenty years, yet mineral collecting is still young and vigorous enough to offer rewarding opportunities for those who join the fastest-growing collecting hobby in America.

Enthusiastic "rockhounds" are to be met today in practically every community. Tens of thousands of adults and youngsters have been attracted to this exciting activity within recent years. You may become a member of a mineral or gem society in almost every state and province, attend regular meetings, and go on conducted field trips to obtain specimens from many interesting localities. Two hundred such clubs exist just in California, many of them providing junior memberships for boys and girls to encourage them in this wholesome and profitable hobby. Most local and state societies are banded together into one of the six regional federations—Eastern, Midwest, Rocky Mountain, Southwest, California, and Northwest— which in turn are affiliated with the American Federation of Mineralogical Societies. These federations sponsor annual conventions, which attract a large attendance to see the extensive exhibits of fellow collectors and dealers who display the newest discoveries and latest equipment. Such a convention is a thrilling spectacle. And there are thousands of equally ardent collectors who do not belong to an organized group but enjoy hunting rocks and minerals just the same.

A hobby that is expanding this fast, appealing to people of all ages and occupations, must possess some strong points. Indeed, mineral collecting does have exceptional advantages to recommend it.

First of all, it is carried on primarily out of doors, where you become acquainted with the wonders and beauties of Nature at her best and learn to understand the expressive face of the earth in its manifold aspects. Scenery is ever-changing, in response to the weathering and erosion of minerals which constitute the rocks of the earth's crust. We find out from a study of minerals why cliffs wear down and how soils originate, why the walls of the Grand Canyon show such vivid hues, why the sands of the Florida beach are so varied in size and shape and color. As the English art critic and author John Ruskin wrote, "There are no natural objects out of which more can be learned than out of stones. They seem to have been created especially to reward a patient observer. For a stone, when it is examined, will be found a mountain in miniature. The surface of a stone is more interesting than the surface of an ordinary hill, more fantastic in form, and incomparably richer in color."

Fig. 1   Emblem of American Federation of Mineralogical Societies

Mineral collecting, furthermore, has its indoor opportunities, even for the shut-in, who can acquire desirable specimens by trading with other collectors and buying from dealers. Splendid selections of minerals are prominently shown in museums in most of the larger cities and in numerous smaller ones, as well as in many colleges and universities. No more pleasant way to spend an evening can be found than in examining the collections of others in your own community or while traveling.

The art of amateur gem cutting, beginning as an off-

Fig. 2   Faceted and cabochon gem cuts

shoot of mineral collecting, has become a major hobby
in itself as thousands of home craftsmen are attaining results superior to those of commercial lapidaries, because
they are eager enough to experiment and persevering
enough to bring their work to a high degree of perfection.
A few of them, endowed with the gift of artistic expres-
sion, turn out carvings of surpassing beauty. Some of
them are able to cut *faceted* stones, having flat surfaces or
"faces" at different angles, while others prefer to make
cabochons, which are simpler because they need only a
rounded top. Enterprising boys, and girls too, using inexpensive equipment, have developed a skill equal to
that of their elders. If you would like to transform stones
into flashing gems, here is the hobby for you.

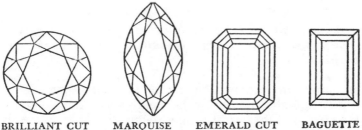

BRILLIANT CUT   MARQUISE   EMERALD CUT   BAGUETTE

Fig. 3   Popular faceted cuts of gems

Crystals, which Abbé Haüy justly called "the flowers
of the minerals," are the chief delight of a large proportion of mineral collectors. Smooth and shining faces,
bright hues, and intriguing forms combine to make crystals outstandingly interesting to those who admire beautiful things. Though scarcely any two crystals seem alike,
we are able to classify them all into six types known as
crystal systems. These are named below, with a model of

11

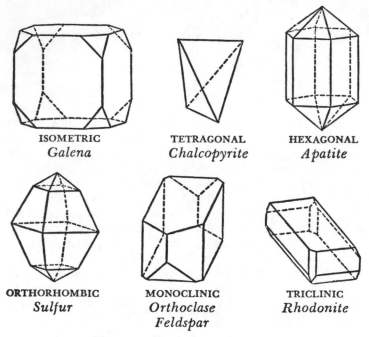

ISOMETRIC	TETRAGONAL	HEXAGONAL
Galena	*Chalcopyrite*	*Apatite*

ORTHORHOMBIC	MONOCLINIC	TRICLINIC
Sulfur	*Orthoclase Feldspar*	*Rhodonite*

Fig. 4   The six crystal systems

A common crystal form or combination of forms is shown for each system. Countless modifications are possible.

an important mineral belonging to each system. They differ from one another in the length and arrangement of the *axes* which run through them; the axes are only imaginary, like the equator and poles of the earth, but are extremely useful in describing crystals.

The most perfect crystals are the smallest ones, because they have been protected by their very smallness. A collection of such miniature crystals or *micromounts,* which are tiny clusters delicately mounted in a box and viewed through a magnifying glass or microscope, reveals a fairyland of breath-taking sparkle and color.

Another phase of mineral collecting that can be carried on indoors is the growing of crystals from saturated chemical solutions. You may cause the crystals to change shape or color in surprising ways by adding a drop of acid or otherwise interfering with the solution as it gives up its dissolved matter.

Few collectors try to accumulate a sample of every mineral or rock; most of them leave to the large museums the task of gathering a comprehensive general collection. Within a short time the beginning collector usually finds out what kind of specimen he likes best and then concentrates on that kind. The most distinctive collections are made by limiting the scope of your efforts and focusing on those that have the greatest appeal to you.

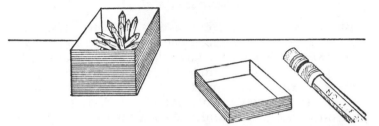

Fig. 5   Micromount, to be observed under magnification

For instance, a collector may specialize in a single mineral—perhaps calcite, which comes in more than 300 different crystal forms; or perhaps quartz, which is abundant everywhere and is found in astonishing variety. Another collector may lean heavily toward ore minerals, of interest particularly to miners and prospectors. Ores of common metals such as iron and copper may be emphasized, or of precious metals such as gold and silver. Minerals from one state or region (perhaps the Rocky Mountains, Death Valley, or New England) or from your home county; minerals of your favorite color; minerals that are finely crystallized; or gem minerals—these likewise are all worthwhile subjects for specialized collections.

An enviable collection might also feature unusual occurrences of minerals, such as *geodes,* which are nodules lined with crystals; or altered minerals called *pseudomorphs* (petrified wood is a good example, the original wood having turned to stone); or sand from rivers and

13

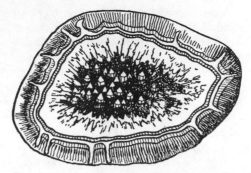

Fig. 6   Geode from Brazil, showing inside lined with amethyst crystals

seashores, or stalactites from caverns, or meteorites which reach the earth from the mysterious vastness of cosmic space. Any of these and many others can be obtained by finding, trading, or buying them. Rocks, either typical ones or curious freaks, and fossils buried in the rocks are appropriately included in a mineral collection. At one time, in fact, minerals and rocks were both called fossils, which in Latin meant "to dig," because they are taken from the earth.

Fig. 7   Stalactite from Mammoth Cave, Kentucky

Mineral collecting can be more than outdoor or indoor fun. It can lead to an acquaintance with one of the most vital sources of human wealth. Mining ranks with farming, fishing, and lumbering as a primary producer of basic raw materials. Man has become dependent upon the mineral industries for the existence of both his peaceful and his military civilizations. Yielding metals, nonmetallic substances, and fuels, our mineral resources largely create the conditions of present-day life on this planet. In addition, minerals have always played an important part in the development of chemistry, physics, and other sciences.

By exposure to the weather, rocks and their minerals decay and fall apart to become soil. Plants are thus able to grow, in turn providing food for animals. Water, which is the most essential of all foods, is also an integral part of the mineral kingdom, being either a rock or a mineral, according to even the most precise definitions.

It is hard to decide which are the most important mineral products besides soil and water. Salt must be included, because it is a mineral indispensable to life—the location of salt licks has marked the route of caravans throughout the centuries. The lure of gems has encouraged trade and transportation since the dawn of history. Flint, a member of the quartz group, was highly prized for weapons, which became the first manufactured articles. Clay, used for pottery, started the earliest large-scale mineral industry. Building stones, as were used in the pyramids, contributed a good deal to the expanding service of earth materials.

Those mentioned above belong among the *nonmetallic* or so-called *industrial minerals and rocks*. The list is seemingly endless, hundreds of them being used in thousands of ways. Consider some more of them—pumice from the Lipari Islands to polish your teeth or from California to insulate your home; potash from New Mexico to fertilize the soil and make farming a scientific employment; emery from Greece to grind away metal in an airplane; asbestos from Quebec to be woven into fireproof clothing; feldspar from North Carolina to glaze chinaware; mica from South Dakota to be flaked into Christmas-tree "snow"; sulfur from Texas to make possible the heavy-chemical industry. Specimens of them all should be represented in your mineral collection.

Coal and petroleum are mineral fuels. Though not so attractive to most collectors, their importance should not be overlooked. Coal is the very foundation of modern industrial economy; countries that lack ample reserves of suitable coal cannot hope to do a large share of the world's manufacturing. Armies, navies, and air forces ride, float, and fly to victory on petroleum.

The *metallic minerals* are the ores from which metals are extracted. These metals may be gold, silver, or platinum—the *precious metals;* or copper, lead, or zinc, which are known as *base metals;* or iron and the so-called *ferroalloy metals,* which are mixed or alloyed with iron to make steel. Discovery of the art of smelting ores revolutionized man's life, enabling him to obtain useful metals from otherwise worthless rock. He could then also melt two or more metals together to produce brass, bronze, and other alloys.

So significant are the mineral products to civilized beings that human history itself is divided into the Old Stone Age, the New Stone Age, the Bronze Age, and the Iron Age. Perhaps we have now moved into the Uranium Age—only the future can tell. As a mineral collector you will be playing your part in the thrilling drama of man.

The amateur collector will probably not come into the fortune of a Texas oilman or of Dr. Williamson, the African diamond magnate, whose faith in his knowledge of the rocks during years of fruitless search was finally repaid by his discovery of the world's largest diamond mine. Nevertheless, the amateur will surely find many fine minerals, perhaps some of satisfying value, and possibly even a new one unknown to science. He will at the same time learn more about his natural environment. Such knowledge is one of the marks of a broadly educated person. And in doing so he will vastly enjoy himself in this vital, many-sided hobby.

More frequently than in the past, hobbyists are turning mineral collecting into a business, selling at a profit to museums, other dealers, and private collectors. Occasionally someone does this as a full-time vocation. The personal experiences of capable professional collectors such as Edwin W. Over, Jr., of Woodland Park, Colo., and Dr. Harvey H. Nininger, the Arizona meteorite expert, in out-of-the-way places ranging from Baja California to Prince of Wales Island off the coast of Alaska, would make entertaining adventure stories.

CHAPTER 2

How Rocks and Minerals Are Formed

The difference between a rock and a mineral should be clearly understood. Rocks are the essential building materials of which the earth is constructed, whereas minerals are the individual substances that go to make up the rocks. Most rocks, therefore, are aggregates of two or more minerals. Thus, granite (a rock) is composed of at least two minerals (quartz and feldspar), though others are almost certain to be present.

If a single mineral exists on a large enough scale, it may also be considered as a rock, because it may then be regarded as an integral part of the structure of the earth. Thus, a pure sandstone or quartzite rock contains only one mineral, quartz, distributed over a wide area. Other single minerals which are described in this book and are regarded also as rocks by this definition include anhydrite, dolomite, gypsum, magnesite, serpentine, and sulfur —all of which occur in huge beds or masses. Some rocks of this type have a different name from that of the mineral composing them. Thus, the mineral halite makes rock salt; calcite is the constituent of the rock called limestone; and either calcite or dolomite can make up the rock called marble. Kaolinite composes many of the rocks we know as clay. Bauxite has been proved to be really a rocky mixture of several minerals, but many geologists still prefer to call it a mineral because of its uniformity.

In addition to these two classifications, rocks include natural glass, though it may be devoid of any actual mineral components. Obsidian, an abundant rock in Mexico and Iceland, is natural volcanic glass. Organic products of the earth, which cannot be called minerals because they are formed from plants and animals, are properly known as rocks. Coal, derived from partly decomposed vegetation, is a rock of this kind.

Seldom will you find a single species of mineral occurring entirely by itself. Like people, minerals have a tend-

17

ency to be found in the company of others of the same kind, having formed under the same conditions. This is a fact which proves most helpful to the collector, who soon discovers that often the best way to recognize a mineral is by its associations.

Thus, feldspar and quartz occur together in the rock called pegmatite because they originate in the same manner, that is, by the cooling of molten rock of a certain chemical composition and within the limited range of temperature required to form pegmatite. Again, no one can fail to know at a glance that he has a specimen of the zinc ore from Franklin, N. J., when he sees the distinctive combination of red zincite, yellowish-green willemite, black franklinite, and white calcite. These minerals are not found together anywhere else in the world, and each mineral immediately suggests the presence of the others. As another instance, in 1870 a man named DeKlerk was led to the first diamond ever recovered from its original rock when he saw some pebbles of garnet in a dry stream bed in South Africa and realized that the two gems often occur side by side.

Moreover, each group of minerals is related naturally to definite types of rock. This enables us to identify the rock more readily than otherwise. Rocks are not so easy to name as minerals because they grade imperceptibly into one another, but this principle of mineral association is very helpful.

The many rocks which constitute the earth's crust are the result of geologic processes acting during long ages, building up some rocks and breaking down others. The normal rock cycle leads from molten rock to igneous rock, then to sediment and sedimentary rock, followed or preceded by a metamorphic stage. Countless bypaths to this cycle give rocks an infinite variety and prevent them from becoming monotonous to anyone who has gained a speaking acquaintance with them and even a slight knowledge of geology.

Igneous Rocks

All minerals and rocks have their primary origin in a body of molten rock called *magma,* which is believed to exist in local pockets deep within the crust of the earth. This magma eventually becomes the igneous rocks and minerals. The name igneous, related to the word *ignite,* suggests fire and heat.

Seismologists, who are the scientists who study earthquake waves, tell us that the earth beneath its relatively thin surface layers is not liquid, as it was formerly thought to be, nor is there outside the core a zone of molten rock. Probably the hot rock is prevented from melting by the enormous pressure upon it, which maintains it in a semiplastic condition. When the pressure is relieved anywhere by cracks in the solid rock above, or heat due to radioactivity reaches the melting temperature, the rock slowly begins to rise in a molten state.

As this magma comes to rest in a cooler place, but still within the earth's crust, it starts to solidify; and thus the igneous rocks are born. They are known as *intrusive* rocks because they have intruded or forced their way into other rocks which were there already. This process has been going on ever since the beginning of geologic time, and so igneous rocks are presumably being formed in the same way today as they have been throughout the long history of our planet.

The intrusive igneous rocks common and important enough to be described in this book are porphyry, granite, pegmatite, syenite, monzonite, gabbro, and peridotite. Constituting the core of mighty mountain chains, these rocks are revealed for observation only after millions of years of prolonged weathering and erosion by the wind and rain and other agents of the atmosphere.

When the molten rock actually breaks through to the surface and wells out as a lava flow, or is blown out as volcanic fragments, the resulting igneous rock is called *extrusive.* We usually have in mind a volcano such as Vesuvius or Mauna Loa when we refer to this sort of igneous rock, but lava can issue quietly from open fissures in the earth without building up a cone or crater, as it still does in Iceland.

More than 500 volcanoes have erupted within recorded history. It is hardly safe to say that a volcano is extinct, for it may only be dormant, waiting for an occasion to awaken once again. Lassen Peak, sleeping in the California Sierras, surprised the nation in 1914 by becoming the only active volcano in the United States. When Vesuvius sprang to life in A.D. 79, suffocating Pompeii and Herculaneum in its grip, it had been so long quiescent that its old activity had been forgotten by the Roman people.

Although volcanoes are widespread throughout the world, the most striking feature of their distribution is the so-called ring of fire surrounding the Pacific Ocean basin, from the tip of South America north to Alaska and back down to New Zealand. Another belt of volcanoes roughly follows the equator from the West Indies to the Mediterranean and on to the East Indies.

The extrusive igneous rocks included in this book are obsidian, pumice, felsite, and basalt. Formed upon the surface or at a shallow depth beneath a light covering, these rocks need not wait long before weathering and erosion set in upon them. The term *vulcanism,* however, includes the behavior of all molten rock, whether it takes place on the surface or far below and whether or not it builds up a typical volcanic mountain with an opening in the center. The originator of this extensive activity was thought to be the Roman god of fire, Vulcan, who operated his workshop underneath glowing Etna, one of the natural lighthouses of the Mediterranean.

Intrusive and extrusive igneous rocks are unlike chiefly because they have cooled at different rates. Intrusive rocks, losing their heat slowly while beneath the ground, acquire a coarse texture as the individual minerals have time to grow to a considerable size. Observe, for instance, the conspicuous pink feldspar, white quartz, and black hornblende in the granite from Pikes Peak. The slowest-cooling igneous rock is pegmatite, and its constituent minerals may be enormous—single crystals of spodumene 20 feet long and muscovite mica 10 feet across.

On the other hand, extrusive rocks cool rapidly; many grains get started, but each is small. Compare even the normal texture of granite, as described above, with the dense basaltic lava of the Columbia Plateau in Oregon, Washington, and Idaho.

In extreme cases of sudden chilling, no minerals are visible at all, the only product being a natural glass. Obsidian Cliff in Yellowstone National Park, seen by a million tourists annually, is a world-famous example of volcanic glass which originated in this fashion. A porous texture, especially of pumice, results from the escape of gas as it bubbles into the air.

Igneous rocks, such as granite and felsite, that are rich in silicon tend to be light-colored and relatively light in weight. As the amount of silicon is reduced and the proportion of iron and magnesium increases, the igneous rocks become darker and heavier, as gabbro and basalt are.

The cooling of magma to form an igneous rock is accompanied by shrinkage and the development of parallel open cracks called *joints*.

Shrinkage also causes cavities or pockets, and these may later be filled or lined with crystals projecting toward the center. Some of the man-sized pockets of this sort yield large gemmy crystals of quartz, feldspar, and other minerals.

Another phase of igneous activity that concerns the mineral collector has to do with ore deposits. Metal-bearing solutions of many kinds accompany the rise of magmas. As the molten rock cools and becomes solid, large quantities of liquid and gas, charged with mineral matter, are given off. Leaving the igneous rocks behind them, they make their way slowly toward the surface, forming mineral deposits wherever conditions are favorable. Thus, lower temperature, reduced pressure, the presence of limestone and other easily changed rocks are conducive to the deposition of ore minerals.

During the long-distance migration of the solutions that have been expelled from the magma, ore deposits of gold, silver, lead, zinc, and other metals are produced. These are referred to as *veins* because they run through

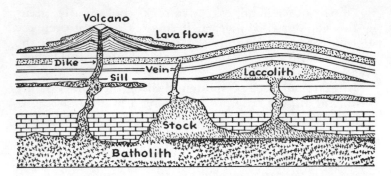

*Fig. 8   Cross section through the earth, showing bodies
in which igneous rock occurs*

the enclosing rock like veins within the skin. They are
classified according to the temperature and pressure at
which they came into existence, which in turn depend
upon the distance they have traveled from the magma.

Eventually, if not used up by one of the processes just
described, the mineral matter that is left may appear at
the surface of the earth in a volcano, gas vent, geyser, or
hot spring. Around the volcanoes of the Mediterranean
shore, for instance, are coatings of such minerals as native
sulfur, realgar, and hematite, which are described in this
book. Amidst the spectacular *fumaroles* or gas vents of
the Valley of Ten Thousand Smokes in Alaska are magnetite, pyrite, galena, and other minerals in large
amounts. The geysers of New Zealand carry gold, silver,
and mercury. Hot water at Steamboat Springs, Nev., is
depositing cinnabar today as in the past. There are
numerous similar examples of each of these mineral occurrences, representing the final stages of igneous activity.

Sedimentary Rocks

Even the most deeply buried igneous rock may someday
be exposed by erosion. The age of the earth, determined
by the measurement of radioactivity in igneous rocks to be
more than three and one-half billion years old, allows ample time for very extensive erosion to have occurred al-

most everywhere. The forces of weathering will then begin to attack the rock, causing it to crumble and decompose. Some of the fine particles may be dissolved by rain water as it seeps through the soil and into the pores of the bedrock underneath. The rest may be washed away bodily by streams, or wafted by the wind, or carried in the frozen grip of giant glaciers.

When either the dissolved rock matter or the transported sediment is deposited somewhere else and afterward hardens into firm rock, we have a sedimentary rock, the second of the two major kinds of rock. Two types of sedimentary rock are possible, according to whether the original material had been dissolved in water or had been moved in the form of fragments.

In the first case—represented by such rocks as rock salt in Kansas and Michigan and beds of borax in Death Valley, Calif.—the minerals are deposited when the dissolving power of the solution is reduced. This may happen because the water gets cooler or some of it evaporates or because of the action of certain plants and animals which extract chemicals from the water. In the same fashion sugar settles at the bottom of the cup when coffee cools, and salt incrusts the sides of a pan when salty water or brine is evaporated.

The second type of sedimentary rock is built up by the accumulation of separate grains of mud, sand, or gravel. Thus, mud becomes shale, sand becomes sandstone, and gravel becomes conglomerate. These sediments vary considerably in their mineral composition, and they grade into one another in the size of their particles.

Although the importance of wind and glaciers as transporting agents cannot be denied, most sedimentary material is nevertheless carried by streams. Rivers are therefore not only the great sculptors of the landscape and the chief creators of scenery, but they likewise play the major role in transporting the products of the earth that are to become the sedimentary minerals and rocks.

Probably the most intriguing sedimentary deposits are the ones known as *placers,* in which are concentrated gold, gems, and other heavy, durable minerals. The bearded Western prospector, equipped with gold pan and accompanied by his faithful burro, is the symbol of placer mining. Resisting chemical decay and physical damage alike, heavy minerals that will end in placers are washed from the higher elevations and taken downstream, until the force of the water is no longer sufficient to move them any farther. A slight obstruction in the channel or change in the current may be enough to cause them to drop to the bottom.

Billions of dollars' worth of native gold has been recovered from the bonanza placers of California, the Klondike, and elsewhere. Besides gold and a number of valuable gem stones—such as diamond, corundum (ruby and sapphire), spinel, and zircon—the most likely constituents of placers include magnetite, chromite, ilmenite, and cassiterite. Quartz, of course, is ever-present.

A special kind of placer is laid down along ocean beaches by waves and shore currents, which effectively separate the heavy minerals from the light ones. At Nome, Alaska, two submerged beaches and four now elevated above sea level have yielded a good deal of gold in very tiny grains. Vast accumulations of ilmenite, rutile, and zircon line the beaches of India, Brazil, Australia, and Florida. So-called *black sands,* containing magnetite, ilmenite, and chromite, are extensively developed on the coasts of California, Oregon, and Japan. A most extraordinary representative of beach placers is the rich diamond bed near Alexander Bay in Namaqualand, South Africa, where diamonds brought down by the Orange River were distributed along the beach, in close association with oyster shells.

Wind often blows the smaller rock fragments into heaps called *dunes.* A single sample of dune sand may contain several dozen different minerals, but they are not of specimen interest except to collectors of sand who must study them under magnification.

Owing to their bulk, glaciers are effective agents in transporting and depositing sediments. Unlike streams and wind, they are not selective in their action, so that a glacier embraces in its icy grasp boulders the size of a house, surrounded by particles that have been ground so relentlessly as to deserve the name "rock flour." With equal disregard for size, a glacier dumps the large and small material at the same time, with no attempt at sorting it. Such accumulations, common in every area glaciated during the recent Ice Age, are called *moraines*. Incorporated in moraines are minerals and rocks of foreign extraction which have been pushed, dragged, or carried bodily from their place of origin, in some cases hundreds of miles away. Chunks of native copper, brought down from the Upper Peninsula of Michigan, are strewn from southern Iowa to Ohio. Masses of chalcocite are frozen in a moraine at Kennecott, Alaska.

Fig. 9   Stratification (horizontal) and joints (vertical) in sedimentary rock, limestone in Indiana

Loose sediment, whatever its origin, eventually becomes solid—"as hard as a rock"—because mineralized underground water cements together the individual grains and the weight of later sediments squeezes down upon them more and more tightly. At a fairly shallow depth, except in arid climates, the ground is saturated with water which fills all pore spaces of the soil and bedrock. This water drains into streams or soaks out at the surface as seeps and springs. In caverns stalactites hang from the roofs, while stalagmites build up from the floors—both the result of evaporation of underground water as it percolates into the earth.

The distinctive property of most sedimentary rocks is their *stratification,* which refers to the layers or beds as each one is deposited on top of the earlier ones. Just as

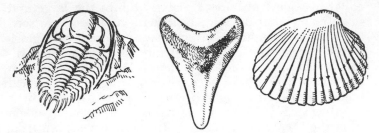

TRILOBITE TOOTH OF ANCIENT SHARK PELECYPOD SHELL

Fig. 10 Common fossils in sedimentary rock

the bottom book in a pile must have been the first one put down, so the lowest bed was the first one deposited, and each successive bed was formed at a later time.

Only in sedimentary rocks are fossils common. The heat of an igneous rock would consume most of the evidence of animal or plant life that might have existed.

Another characteristic of sedimentary rocks is the presence of foreign lumps or nodules called *concretions*. In the white cliffs of Dover are numerous odd-shaped pieces of flint, perhaps secreted by ancient sponges when the chalk that now makes up the cliffs was deposited in a shallow sea.

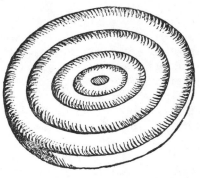

Fig. 11 Concretion from shale bed, Virginia

Joints are as abundant in sedimentary rocks as they are in igneous rocks, but the shrinkage which causes them is the result of drying instead of cooling. Most sediments are laid down in water—streams, lakes, the ocean—and may contain 50 per cent or more of moisture, some of which is driven off during burial.

The sedimentary rocks described in this book are conglomerate, coal, shale, limestone, and sandstone.

Metamorphic Rocks

The third main kind of rock, called *metamorphic,* is the result of drastic changes in either an igneous or a sedimentary rock. The new rock has been changed so much from its original state that practically all signs of ancient life are gone, and so fossils are almost never present. Even most of the evidence as to the nature of the original rock has been lost, and often it is impossible to tell whether the preexisting rock was igneous or sedimentary.

Heat from an invading magma that forces its way toward the surface of the earth is one of the factors that produces a metamorphic rock by creating new textures or entirely new minerals from the old rock. Another factor is pressure resulting from deep burial or slow movement in the earth's crust, pressure of the sort that ultimately bends rocks into mountain ranges. The chemical action of liquids and gases is also effective.

Limestone, for example, turns from a sedimentary rock into marble as the grains of calcite recrystallize under the influence of the agents of metamorphism. Because of the recrystallization, marble usually has a more glistening appearance than limestone. New minerals may be formed in the process, giving marble the swirled patterns that are so attractive a feature of colored marble. The collector may expect to find garnet, idocrase, and epidote, among many other minerals characteristic of this type of occurrence. Scheelite, an ore of tungsten, is perhaps the most valuable metallic mineral originating in this manner.

Joints are prominent in metamorphic rocks, for the gradual but irresistible application of natural forces strains them past the breaking point.

The metamorphic rocks described in this book are gneiss, schist, slate, marble, and quartzite.

Soils and Scenery

The weathering of any of these three major types of rock leads to the formation of soil. In addition to broken fragments of decomposing rock, soil consists of decayed plant material. With continued weathering, the soil zone becomes deeper and the bedrock further concealed. New minerals are created in this process, but with few exceptions they are scarcely suitable as specimens. Some of the chemical elements in the soil combine into various soluble compounds which, when they are washed out of the ground, leave the soil depleted of elements essential to plant growth.

As important to the natural history of rocks and minerals as the making of soil and the production of ore deposits is the creation of the scenery that beautifies and diversifies our terrestrial environment. The inhabitants of the earth during much of geologic time—if there had been any thinking beings prior to our own brief age— would have lived on a monotonous globe. Often devoid of mountains and hills, glaciers and volcanoes, the earth throughout a large part of its existence has been a desolate place. When the seas inundated the low-lying continents, they spread widely over the dreary landscape. When they retreated, they left behind an even more barren scene. At irregular intervals, of course, majestic mountain ranges pushed their way into the sky, thick masses of glacial ice inched precarious paths down the frosty slopes, and volcanoes spewed forth flaming debris upon the horizon.

But these momentous events only made the dismalness of the intervening periods seem the more uninspiring by contrast. We are more fortunate than perhaps we deserve to live in a world only lately having suffered the paroxysms of mountain building, only recently emerging from an Ice Age which has crowned its higher elevations with shining diadems of white.

What scenery comes into view in any given place at any given time depends upon the underlying rock and

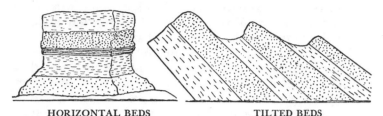

HORIZONTAL BEDS   TILTED BEDS

Fig. 12 Difference in topography caused by structure

the kind of geologic agent acting upon it. Hard limestone, for instance, may stand erect as a sharp cliff, while a crumbly shale next to it will disintegrate into a rolling valley. Whereas flat layers of durable sandstone will protect from erosion the softer beds between them, thereby forming a mesa or butte, the same association of rocks will appear as alternating hills and valleys if the layers have been tilted on edge.

Blowing sand fashions scenery in a desert region unlike that of underground water in an area noted for its caves. Ocean breakers are responsible for scenic effects very different from those caused by the pull of gravity as it sets into motion landslides and avalanches.

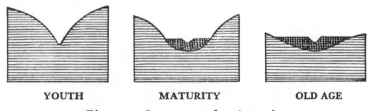

YOUTH   MATURITY   OLD AGE

Fig. 13 Stream cycle of erosion

Even the same agent of erosion or deposition avoids uniformity by taking its scenery through a cycle. Rivers, for instance, go from a youthful stage to one of maturity, then into old age. As the cycle progresses, the valley assumes new characteristics which enable the experienced observer to recognize the relative age of that particular stream. The sharp V-shaped valley of a youthful stream gives way to one having a flatter profile as the river cuts its way downward and sideward. The development of

29

meanders accentuates the swing of the stream until, in old age, it wanders across a wide valley between low hills.

To the person with a vivid and inquiring mind, the rocks and the minerals in them are never static things. They come into the earth's crust in numerous ways, they are transformed into many new substances, and they undergo experiences that challenge the imagination. And they never cease to exist in one form or another. To such an alert person who also knows the dramatic story of the rocks and minerals, they are not only seen in three dimensions and in color but they acquire the fourth dimension of time.

CHAPTER 3

Building a Mineral Collection

A mineral and rock collection is as near as your back yard and as distant as the far corners of the world. Specimens of some members of the mineral kingdom may be secured with little trouble and less cost, while others require the initiative of a globe-trotter and the purse of a merchant prince. Minerals are to be found in garden soil, in road cuts and building excavations, under cliffs and in stream beds, on beaches and sand dunes, in quarries and mines. Heaps of waste rock called *dumps* are a prolific source of specimens. Everywhere around us, in fact, minerals are present.

Cavities in rock are especially favorable spots for finding choice crystals, for in such open spaces they have a chance to grow freely to substantial sizes. Ordinary-looking boulders known as geodes, when broken open, often reveal rows of glistening crystals lining the inner walls, like the inside of a treasure cave in a storybook. Mammoth crystal-filled geodes, outwardly resembling the eggs of some prehistoric beast, are picked up by the thousands around Keokuk, Iowa, and elsewhere in the central Mississippi Valley.

A small number of minerals can be sifted as pebbles from the soil in one's own yard. Sand and clay pits and other diggings in soft rock will yield additional interesting minerals, among them fine specimens of gypsum, pyrite, and marcasite. Near exposed cliffs and rock outcrops, road and railway cuts and tunnels in solid rock, and excavations made for the construction of buildings are promising places to search for minerals. Quarries and coal mines are common, and their waste piles may be surprisingly productive. An intriguing feature of coal deposits is the abundance of fossils—the remains or impressions of plants and animals that once lived on the earth. Monument works, which are often situated in the vicinity of quarries, are worth a visit, and so are smelters.

The best sources of minerals are, of course, mines and their dumps. In the United States, mines are not limited, as you may have believed, to the open spaces of the West. On the contrary, Pennsylvania, West Virginia, Illinois, Kentucky, and Ohio stand among the eight leading mineral-producing states. Two of the largest zinc mines in the country are near Ogdensburg, N.J., within 40 miles of the metropolis of New York City, and in St. Lawrence County, N.Y.

The loose sand and sagebrush areas of deserts yield— besides agate and other minerals usually expected there —flowerlike groups of crystals, including the attractive "desert roses" and "barite roses." The temporary lakes in arid regions give up halite, borax, and many other saline minerals, which form when the water evaporates. Beach sands may contain a multitude of heavy minerals brought together by waves and currents from widespread localities. Owing their origin to the uplift of a mountain range, the explosion of a volcano, the flow of lava, the bubbling of a hot spring, even the crash of a shooting star, the products of the mineral kingdom are on every hand.

Mineral localities consequently are world-wide. Many specimens are available on public land, especially in the national forests; the national parks and monuments, except Death Valley, are closed to collecting. Others can often be obtained on private property by asking permission and taking care to close gates and respect the rights of the owners or residents.

You might consider seriously the size of the specimens you want to collect. Some collectors, having unlimited space, feature large and showy specimens, whereas others are obliged to restrict themselves to micromounts, the exquisite miniature crystals which occupy little more room than a stamp or coin collection. Either extreme is perfectly acceptable, though the average collector acquires whatever pleases his fancy, regardless of size, and seems always to need more room than is available. The number of specimens of the same kind to be taken is also a matter of decision. It is true that duplicate ones can usually be traded off, and even sold, but it is the excessively greedy collector who gives the hobby a bad name—he and the fellow who despoils other people's property.

If the specimens finally admitted to your collection are chosen with discrimination, the result will be a genuinely valuable asset. Each of the kinds of materials described in this book—minerals, gems, ores, crystals, rocks, meteorites —can be assembled into a handsome, interesting, and profitable collection. Sands, pebbles, concretions, geodes, stalactites and stalagmites, and many other forms are also proper specialties around which to build a collection. The list is extensive, making possible enough variety to suit the taste of almost every person who has an interest in the wonders of inorganic nature.

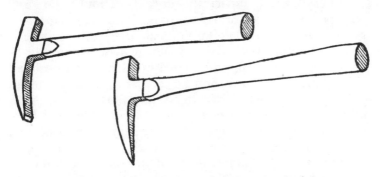

Fig. 14   Prospector's hammer and pick

A mineral collector does not require elaborate equipment, but he may make or buy as much as he needs for certain purposes. The one essential item in the field is a prospector's hammer, with either a pick or a chisel opposite the hammer head. A sledge hammer, light or heavy, will sometimes be worth taking along, especially if it does not need to be carried far. A separate cold chisel is also useful for wedging rock apart or freeing crystals from crevices. Square-pointed and diamond-pointed steel tools are additional equipment for extracting specimens. Excess rock may be trimmed away with the same sudden but carefully planned blows used in the mining operation itself; a succession of light taps is usually as effective as one hard blow and is more easily controlled.

33

Fig. 15   Collector's knapsack

Minerals, and especially crystals, should be well wrapped in cotton or tissue paper and newspaper, together with a paper label giving adequate information as to locality and identity, if known. Adhesive tape can be used to attach a temporary label or identifying number. The specimens should then be carried in a cloth, canvas, or leather knapsack. Delicate crystals, particularly, ought to be protected against the hazards of transportation, which cause more damage to even the toughest rocks than does anything else. Gloves to wear while working, a magnifying glass for examining small specimens, a notebook to record your observations, a field guide like this one, a camera, and a pocketknife are other desirable articles to have. Inexpensive things such as an ice pick, a file, and a ruler often come in handy. Adequate clothing should be

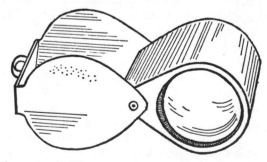

Fig. 16   Collector's pocket magnifying lens

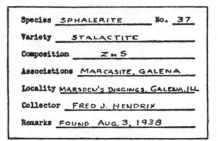

Species _SPHALERITE_   No. _37_

Variety _STALACTITE_

Composition _Z n S_

Associations _MARCASITE, GALENA_

Locality _MARSDEN'S DIGGINGS, GALENA, ILL_

Collector _FRED J. HENDRIX_

Remarks _FOUND AUG. 3, 1938_

Fig. 17   Mineral label

Fig. 18   Rock label

Name _RHYOLITE PORPHYRY_ No. _16_

Occurrence _SIDE OF MESA_

Locality _HOLDEN GULCH, near BELMONT, NEW_

Collector _WILLIAM BURNS_

Remarks _EXCHANGED FOR JASPER_

worn, just as for any type of outing or camp life. Testing apparatus is described later in this book, but identification is usually best made at your leisure at home or in a laboratory.

Specimens should be trimmed carefully to size, but without destroying the surrounding matrix of a crystal; a pink topaz crystal in light-gray rhyolite from the Thomas Range of Utah, for instance, is of more interest and brings a higher price than the loose crystal, because it shows the natural occurrence and associations. Another reason for the greater value of a matrix specimen of topaz is that it is less common than an isolated crystal. This is true of nearly every mineral.

Good grooming will improve a mineral specimen. Most specimens can be cleaned in soapy warm water applied with a soft brush. Soluble minerals, such as halite (table salt), cannot, of course, be immersed in water, but alcohol will rinse them. A blast of air will remove dust from fragile specimens such as the hairlike zeolites. A coating of clear lacquer may aid in protecting specimens from soil or tarnish. Each mineral has an individuality of its own, and the technique of cleaning and preserving mineral specimens may require some time to learn.

After cleaning them, you may give your specimens a permanent label by writing or typing the data on adhesive tape or lettering them in india ink on a patch of white enamel painted on the surface. Most collectors like to prepare a simple paper or cardboard label which will stand or lie next to each specimen and show the essential information about it. If this is done, the specimen itself need bear only an accession number beginning with 1; a small label of this sort provides a neater-looking specimen but makes necessary some kind of cataloguing system. Therefore, the specimens are finally enumerated and described in a notebook or card file. An index or cross-reference list is desirable for finding quickly all specimens of a given kind or from a given locality. The sample labels on page 35 tell the least that should generally be known about a mineral or a rock.

Fig. 19   Mineral cabinet with partitioned drawers

At first you may use simple storage boxes until your collection expands and you feel the need of a good case to set off some of your really beautiful specimens. M. F. Wasson, a Denver attorney, has demonstrated an example of the ingenuity possible in displaying minerals to the best advantage, by illuminating an old china cabinet with concealed strings of white Christmas-tree lights. Some collectors who are wealthy or skilled in carpentry have built-in wall cases in their homes or have bought standard metal floor cases of the kind seen in museums. Portable outfits resembling a traveling salesman's sample case and consisting of removable sliding trays, which can

Fig. 20   Riker mount with glass top

be set on a table, are popular with collectors who own them.

Gems and small crystals are easy to exhibit in Riker mounts, which are frames that come in various dimensions; being paper-bound and glass-covered, they can be handled without danger of damaging the contents and can be suspended from a wall like pictures. Attractive plastic boxes and more elaborate wood frames are coming into the market, as interest in the mineral hobby expands. Larger specimens can be mounted on individual stands of metal, wood, glass, or plastic; besides being transparent, plastic can be attractively lettered with a vibrating electric tool. There is no end to the possibilities in housing,

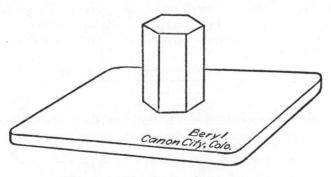

Fig. 21   Plastic specimen mount

lighting, mounting, arranging, and labeling a mineral collection for display.

Unless you are fortunate enough to be able to travel extensively on every continent and collect all the specimens you want, you will sooner or later realize the benefit to your collection of well-selected purchases. Dealers who advertise in the magazines named on page 187 have world-wide connections, enabling you to have eventually a thoroughly representative collection. Also, you will learn faster by having at hand an inexpensive selection of named samples to study and test. An increasing number of dealers maintain regular stores in which browsing and shopping can conveniently be done.

Specimens that you do not find yourself or buy from a dealer may be secured by exchanging with fellow collectors; this is one of the benefits of membership in a club devoted to the mineral hobby. Material to be traded should be clean and well labeled, accompanied by a list giving the pertinent information and particularly the locality. Packages to be shipped by parcel post or express should be well packed, for minerals often prove to be disappointingly fragile.

Growing crystals artificially is becoming increasingly popular. This is a creative activity which is in some ways as satisfying as collecting in the field. It also has its scientific aspects, for it helps us understand the conditions existing in nature that govern the growth of minerals. Copper sulfate, nickel sulfate, potash or chrome alum, Rochelle salt, potassium ferrocyanide, and potassium fer-

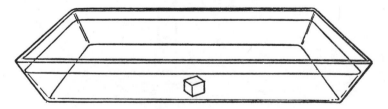

Fig. 22 *Growing artificial crystal*

ricyanide are among the chemical salts that will crystallize readily, requiring only a saturated solution in a flat dish or Mason jar, kept where the temperature is constant and outside interference is at a minimum.

As the solution slowly evaporates, the upper part becomes supersaturated with the dissolved salt. Being denser, it sinks to the bottom of the dish, where it adds its excess salt to the crystal that has already started to grow. Perhaps a seed crystal of the same substance has been placed in the dish for the purpose of encouraging growth. Then the liquid rises again and the process continues over and over, while the crystal increases in size. Larger and more symmetrical crystals are made by suspending a seed crystal on a wire to serve as a nucleus, though the solution may need to be stirred from time to time.

The color of the crystal is often very pretty in itself, such as the deep blue of copper sulfate, the lemon yellow of potassium ferrocyanide, and the ruby red of potassium ferricyanide. It can be varied by adding a small amount of pigment, and wholly colorless crystals take on delicate hues when a drop of ink or dye is put into the solution.

Changes in the shape of the crystal can be effected by adding almost any foreign substance. Small crystals attach themselves to the main one and may have to be removed, after which the larger crystal heals over. A lifetime of interesting experiments awaits the grower of artificial crystals, with something new revealed every day.

Visits to museums are strongly encouraged as a means of becoming familiar with choice specimens. Almost every college and university has a geological museum, and some cities boast truly magnificent exhibits. Among the finest mineral collections on the North American continent are those in the American Museum of Natural History (New York), Harvard University (Cambridge, Mass.), Philadelphia Academy of Natural Sciences, United States National Museum (Washington), Royal Ontario Museum of Mineralogy (Toronto), Chicago Museum of Natural History, Denver Museum of Natural History, and Los Angeles County Museum of History, Science, and Art. In mining regions, especially in the West, local material is often shown in the county courthouses and in the windows of assayers. Before collecting in a given locality, it is wise to look first at specimens of minerals and rocks that have already been found there, in order to be sure of their appearance and names.

At the end of the descriptive section you will find brief notes about books especially recommended for further reading. A small personal library is a source of much satisfaction to the collector as he grows in experience and knowledge. These books contain information on many subjects of interest to mineral and rock collectors, and the locality guides furnish detailed instructions for reaching productive deposits in many states. These and more detailed books can be borrowed through nearly every public and school library, whether or not they actually are on the shelves.

A list of the national magazines dealing with this hobby is also given in this book. A good suggestion is that every serious-minded collector, whether beginner or advanced, should subscribe to one of these periodicals. The instruction and inspiration you will receive will more than repay the small cost.

CHAPTER 4

Seven Keys to Recognizing Minerals

The secret of identifying minerals quickly and successfully is to become familiar with their common physical properties. A property of a substance is any quality typical of it, or anything pertaining to its appearance. Thus, a sweet taste is a property of sugar, a white color is a property of snow, and heaviness is a property of lead.

Unless we can recognize a mineral by sight alone, it may seem to be any one of many minerals, but as soon as we are able to determine one or two definite properties, we have immediately reduced the long list of possible minerals to the names of a few probable ones. With only these to choose from, we can much more easily decide the true identity of the unknown specimen. The convenient arrangement of the Seven Keys used in this book ought to enable you to recognize the most important minerals by an easy step-by-step procedure.

MINERAL KEY NO. 1   LUSTER

Light is reflected from the surface of minerals in various ways, producing a number of different types of luster. First of all, every mineral has either a *metallic* or a *nonmetallic* luster, according to whether or not it resembles the surface of a metal. This serves to put any unknown mineral into one of two main groups without further delay.

A metallic luster, though difficult to describe, is simple to recognize, being the luster of a typical metal—gold, silver, lead, copper, aluminum, and the rest. Minerals having this luster are opaque, and when crushed they yield a powder which is black or darker in color than the mineral itself. (This powder is referred to as *streak* and is described in Key No. 4.)

A nonmetallic luster is more complex, because several kinds can be recognized. Minerals having a nonmetallic luster become transparent on a thin edge, and when crushed they give a powder which is white or lighter in color than the solid mineral.

Perhaps the most common of the nonmetallic lusters is *vitreous,* which means glassy; it is how ordinary glass looks in reflected light. Quartz and many other minerals have this sort of luster. Minerals such as mica that display cleavage (described in Key No. 5) have a *pearly* luster, which is due to closely parallel layers' trapping the light and breaking it up into tiny rainbows. Diamond and nonmetallic lead minerals reflect a brilliant luster called *adamantine,* which means diamondlike. Sphalerite is one of the few minerals which shows a *resinous* luster, like that of rosin from trees. A *silky* luster is displayed by fibrous minerals such as gypsum of the satin-spar variety. *Greasy, oily,* and other lusters may be described in common words just as they appear to the observer.

MINERAL KEY NO. 2   HARDNESS

A rock is often called soft because the individual particles, which may be hard in themselves, are loosely held together and readily fall apart. In speaking of minerals, however, hardness means the resistance of the whole surface to being scratched.

A century ago a mineralogist named Friedrich Mohs devised a scale of hardness which is still in use and known as the *Mohs scale.* He placed talc, the softest of all minerals (soft enough to be made into talcum powder), as No. 1 in this series, and diamond, the hardest of all known substances, as No. 10. The complete scale is given below.

10	Diamond	5	Apatite
9	Corundum	4	Fluorite
8	Topaz	3	Calcite
7	Quartz	2	Gypsum
6	Feldspar	1	Talc

The Mohs scale does not indicate any exact hardness; thus, No. 9 is not three times as hard as No. 3. It means only that any mineral can scratch all those beneath it in

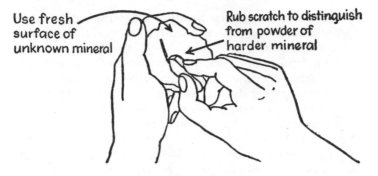

Use fresh surface of unknown mineral

Rub scratch to distinguish from powder of harder mineral

Fig. 23   Testing hardness

the scale and in turn will be scratched by those above it. Two minerals of the same hardness will scratch each other. For convenience, some familiar objects, which enable us to make tests quickly in the field, have been included in the scale, as follows:

2½   Fingernail
3   Copper coin
5½   Knife blade, window glass
6½   Steel file

Minerals under 2½ will leave a mark on paper; those under 5½ can be scratched by a knife; those over 5½ will scratch glass.

MINERAL KEY NO. 3   COLOR

Nature field guides customarily use color as a basis of classification. This is generally true of those dealing with birds, flowers, butterflies, etc., in which color plays a chief part in identification. Minerals, however, are so variable that we can scarcely rely upon color as a satisfactory means of recognizing them.

Some minerals, it is true, are reasonably constant in their color, such as yellow sulfur, pink rhodochrosite, blue azurite, and green malachite. Most minerals, however, are colored by chemical elements that are really minor impurities and that produce a bewildering array of colors without changing the essential composition. Quartz, for instance, occurs in almost every imaginable color, as do tourmaline, corundum, and numerous other minerals. Nevertheless, certain colors are more or less characteristic of particular minerals, and in the following outline and descriptive section they are emphasized whenever they may be useful in identifying the mineral.

You should note that many minerals have a tendency to tarnish somewhat, and so a freshly broken surface may have to be exposed to reveal the true color. This is so dominant a property of the mineral bornite, which miners often call peacock ore and purple copper ore, that bornite is listed here under the usual purple color of its tarnish.

MINERAL KEY NO. 4   STREAK

Most minerals lose their color entirely when they are finely crushed. Some, however, still show a pale color, similar to that of the whole mineral, but lighter. A few

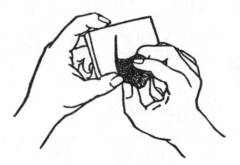

Fig. 24   Testing streak of mineral on streak plate

mineral powders give a fairly vivid color, which may even be rather different from the original one seen before crushing.

The color of a powdered mineral is called its streak because it is usually obtained by rubbing it against a piece of unglazed porcelain. For this purpose ordinary pieces of untreated tile are sold for a few cents as *streak plates,* but the edge of a broken china cup or dish is adequate though not so convenient to handle. One mineral for which streak is a useful property in identification is hematite. No matter how black or steely it may look at first, every piece of hematite gives an Indian-red streak; the name of the mineral, which means "bloodstone," was derived from this fact.

MINERAL KEY NO. 5   CLEAVAGE

Crystalline minerals are said to cleave or have cleavage when they break in definite directions along smooth surfaces. This interesting property is the result of a precise pattern of atoms in regular layers, whose cohesion is weaker in certain directions than in others. A piece of mica will flake into thinner and thinner sheets because it can be so readily cleaved in a single direction. Other minerals have two, three, four, or as many as six directions of cleavage.

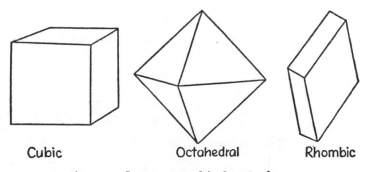

Cubic   Octahedral   Rhombic

Fig. 25   Important kinds of cleavage

Cleavage is often confused with an original crystal face, though the pearly luster of the cleavage surface is a helpful clue. We describe cleavage according to how easily it is obtained and what its crystal direction is. Diamond, for example, has a "perfect octahedral" cleavage, which is used by diamond cutters to remove flawed parts of a crystal merely by splitting them away with a sharp blow.

45

Cleavage is a constant enough property to serve as an excellent means of identifying minerals. It can best be recognized by small steplike surfaces on the outside in preference to internal cracks, because these may be due to other causes.

When a mineral breaks with smooth surfaces like those of cleavage but only in certain favored places and on only a few specimens, it is said to show pseudocleavage, or *parting*. Because true cleavage and parting resemble each other so closely, they are included together in the outline and descriptive section of this book, though mentioned separately under the individual minerals.

MINERAL KEY NO. 6   FRACTURE

Minerals that break in irregular directions, like shattered glass, are said to fracture instead of cleave. The particular kind of fracture depends upon the appearance of the new surface. When it has a series of arcs, typical of the growth pattern of shells, it is known as *conchoidal*, meaning shell-like. Quartz and a host of other minerals have this con-

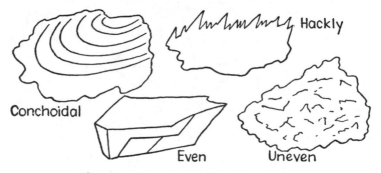

Fig. 26   Important kinds of fracture

choidal fracture, which is also seen on chipped glass. Native metals such as copper and silver have a *hackly* fracture, which gives a jagged surface uncomfortable to touch. Other kinds of fracture are called simply *even, uneven, earthy,* and so forth—ordinary words that describe their appearance.

Minerals vary considerably in weight, some being heavy for their size, others light. The relative weight of a mineral is known as its specific gravity, which is a number that gives a direct comparison with the weight of an equal volume of water. For instance, a specimen of corundum having a specific gravity of 4.0 weighs four times as much as the same volume of water.

Methods for determining specific gravity are beyond the scope of this book, but experience in handling specimens will give you a surprising ability to estimate it closely. A typical metallic mineral such as pyrite or hematite has a specific gravity of about 5. A typical nonmetallic mineral has a specific gravity between 2.6 and 2.8, a range which covers the common minerals quartz, feldspar, and calcite. Minerals appreciably above or below these values seem noticeably heavy or light when lifted. These average figures are used as the basis of distinction in the outline and descriptive section of this book. Thus, a specimen which might be of medium weight for a metallic mineral would perhaps be considered heavy for a nonmetallic mineral—your own judgment and experience tell you what to expect when you lift it.

OTHER MINERAL PROPERTIES

Minerals possess a wide range of physical properties besides those described above as the Seven Keys to Mineral Recognition. Whenever any of these properties is typical of a given mineral and is therefore a valuable clue for identifying it, you will find the property described or illustrated in the descriptive section of this book. The more common and useful of these miscellaneous properties are discussed here now.

Many minerals belonging to the carbonate class will effervesce, or fizz, in acid, a reaction involving the escape of carbon dioxide gas. Household vinegar is sufficiently strong, though you will often find it helpful to scratch the specimen with a knife blade to form a powder which reacts more quickly. Dilute hydrochloric (muriatic) acid is the standard acid for this purpose. Of the minerals described in this book, the following are carbonates: aragonite, azurite, calcite, cerussite, dolomite, magnesite, malachite, rhodochrosite, siderite, smithsonite, strontianite. Some of these react more slowly than others, and some satisfactorily only when the solution is warmed. The only one that needs a different acid to dissolve it is cerussite which requires nitric acid to give the proper effect. If anything stronger than vinegar is used, it should be handled carefully and carried in a bottle having an eye dropper or glass rod attached to the stopper for convenience in touching it to the specimen.

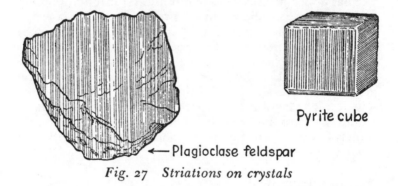

Pyrite cube

←—Plagioclase feldspar

Fig. 27   Striations on crystals

Striations are parallel straight lines resembling a grating. They come about in several different ways. Some mark the boundary between the parts of twin crystals, where the twinning is repeated over and over again. This sort of striation is seen on plagioclase feldspar. Others, as shown on pyrite and quartz, result from a conflict between two kinds of crystal faces, each controlling the growth for a while and one of them finally winning out.

Flexible minerals, such as chlorite, can be bent in your fingers and will stay bent until forced in another direction. *Elastic* minerals, on the contrary, will snap back to their original position unless they have actually been

48

broken; the mica minerals are typical examples of this interesting property.

Malleable minerals are those which can be hammered flat without falling to powder. The native metals—gold, silver, copper—are malleable, though loosely held fragments sometimes crumble or come apart. *Sectile* minerals can be cut with a knife, like horn or dry cheese, without powdering, but they will pulverize if pounded with a hammer. A few minerals described in this book, such as gypsum, are somewhat sectile.

Magnetic minerals are those which can be attracted by a common horseshoe or bar magnet. After being heated, or when tested with an electromagnet, hundreds of minerals are magnetic, but only two of the common minerals —magnetite and pyrrhotite—can be picked up before such treatment.

Fig. 28   Short-wave ultraviolet lamp

Fluorescent minerals glow in the dark when exposed to invisible radiation, such as ultraviolet light, X rays, and cathode rays. The most practicable source for such radiation is an *ultraviolet lamp,* which may be of two main types. The long-wave lamp emits a good deal of heat. The short-wave lamp, though more expensive, is cool and it is effective with a larger number of minerals. Either one causes colors to appear that were not perceptible before. A glass filter is employed to screen out the undesirable visible light, but a dull purple almost always comes through. Some of the most spectacular optical effects in the mineral kingdom are obtained by fluorescence.

When the glow continues after the lamp is turned off, the mineral is said to be *phosphorescent*. Other kinds of so-called *luminescence* can be produced by heating or striking certain minerals in the dark. Although fluorite is the mineral which gave its name to the property, it does not show fluorescence as well as some others. Of the ones described in this book, scheelite and willemite can be most relied upon to show fluorescence. Many diamonds fluoresce, and so do many specimens of calcite and opal. Battery-powered portable lamps have been a popular item of equipment for prospecting for scheelite, an important ore of tungsten.

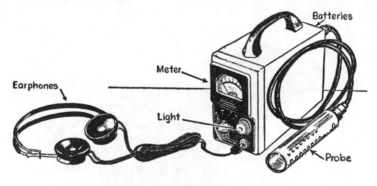

Fig. 29   Portable Geiger counter

Radioactive minerals break down spontaneously and at a uniform rate. As the atoms disintegrate and change to other elements, they give off energy. Although various kinds of equipment will detect this radiation, the instrument most generally in use is the *Geiger counter*. By means of a click, a flashing bulb, or a dial, the presence of the invisible radiation is revealed. Portable models have become common among prospectors, both professional and amateur. Pitchblende (or uraninite) and carnotite are the radioactive minerals described in this book, although zircon and a few others often possess this vital property to a minor extent.

The ability of some minerals such as enargite and stibnite to *fuse* or melt in the flame of a match or candle is worth remarking upon. Cryolite is unique among the minerals included in this book in its property of becoming virtually invisible when immersed in water, because there is very little difference in the light-bending power of the mineral and the liquid.

Final identification of a difficult mineral might require blowpipe tests, chemical tests or analyses, optical examination with a petrographic microscope, or X-ray photography. Such procedures are explained in the more advanced textbooks on mineralogy.

How to Read Chemical Formulas

The chemical composition of minerals is written in a special shorthand called a formula, which is really quite simple to read. It tells which chemical elements go to make up the mineral and how many atoms there are of each kind. For example, the formula of quartz is SiO_2, denoting that this mineral is composed of silicon (Si) and oxygen (O), the proportion being one atom of silicon to two atoms of oxygen. Every chemical element is given a symbol which is an abbreviation of either the English or the Latin name. Thus, C stands for carbon, Ca for calcium, and Fe for *ferrum,* which means iron. The symbols of forty of the most common elements occurring in minerals are included in the following list. Those marked with an asterisk (*) are able to exist by themselves as native elements or minerals in the earth's crust; more than half of them are common or important enough to be described in this book. The rest of the elements listed below are combined with other elements in the form of mineral *compounds.*

* Ag	Silver		Ba	Barium
Al	Aluminum		Be	Beryllium
* As	Arsenic		* Bi	Bismuth
* Au	Gold		* C	Carbon
B	Boron		Ca	Calcium

51

Cl	Chlorine	Ni	Nickel
Cr	Chromium	O	Oxygen
Co	Cobalt	P	Phosphorus
• Cu	Copper	• S	Sulfur
F	Fluorine	Si	Silicon
• Fe	Iron	• Sb	Antimony
H	Hydrogen	Sn	Tin
• Hg	Mercury	Sr	Strontium
K	Potassium	Te	Tellurium
Li	Lithium	Ti	Titanium
• Pb	Lead	U	Uranium
Mg	Magnesium	V	Vanadium
Mn	Manganese	W	Tungsten
Mo	Molybdenum	Zn	Zinc
Na	Sodium	Zr	Zirconium

Certain *radicals,* or combinations of elements, are especially frequent in minerals. These belong to various major chemical classes, of which the most important are listed here, with an example of each, taken from this book.

Al_2O_4	Aluminate	Spinel
B_4O_7, etc.	Borate	Borax
CO_3	Carbonate	Calcite
Cr_2O_4	Chromite	Chromite
MoO_4	Molybdate	Wulfenite
PO_4	Phosphate	Apatite
SO_4	Sulfate	Barite
SiO_4, Si_2O_6,		
Si_3O_8, etc.	Silicate	Zircon
TiO_2	Titanate	Ilmenite
VO_4	Vanadate	Vanadinite
WO_4	Tungstate	Scheelite

Other chemical classes, consisting of a single element, which combines with one or more different elements, include the following:

As	Arsenide	Niccolite
Cl	Chloride	Halite
F	Fluoride	Fluorite
O_2	Oxide	Hematite
S	Sulfide	Galena

Water may be present in the form of H_2O, as in gypsum, or as hydroxyl (OH), as in topaz. The oxide of silicon (SiO_2) is referred to simply as silica. When a formula includes a comma, as (Fe,Al), it means that the given atom may be of either element (here, iron or aluminum, as in epidote). The letter n, as nH_2O in opal, indicates a variable number of groups of atoms.

How to Use the Outlines

Through a step-by-step process of eliminating the classifications that do not apply to the specimen you are trying to name, you ought to arrive at the section which includes the right mineral. A few precautions, however, may prove of value.

If you are not certain about the existence of any one of the properties upon which the outline is based, you will be wise to examine either the opposite section or the adjacent ones. For example, if the cleavage is probably present but appears indistinct, try the sections headed "Shows good cleavage" and "Does not show good cleavage." If the other properties are sure but the hardness is doubtful, examine the sections varying in hardness from the one you have almost decided upon. This technique holds good for luster, color, and streak as well—of these, the streak is most apt to cause uncertainty.

Each section begins with the minerals that are generally most easily recognized by their typical color or other readily observed characteristics. This facilitates identifying the more difficult minerals, because once the simpler ones are eliminated, attention can be confined to the details of the less obvious ones.

A magnifying glass should be used to examine the cleavage, striations, inclusions, or other features shown in the drawings because they may be present on too small a scale to be visible otherwise.

The color is indicated in the illustrations for those minerals which belong to groups whose color is used as a key for classifying them. For the rest the chief colors are given in the scientific data above the illustrations.

Bornite is placed according to the purple color of its tarnish, which is the hue almost always seen. The other minerals are classified by the color of their fresh surface, although the outside of the specimen is often somewhat darkened or made iridescent by a film of tarnish. Hence a newly broken surface should be exposed before deciding the color, especially of a metallic mineral.

Identifying the Minerals. Outline of Keys

A. Metallic luster   *Page* 56
 1. Can mark paper   *Page* 56
   a. Blue color   *Page* 56
   b. Gray or black color   *Page* 57
 2. Cannot mark paper, but can be scratched by knife blade   *Page* 62
   a. Copper color   *Page* 62
   b. Purple color   *Page* 68
   c. Red or brown color   *Page* 69
   d. Gray or black color   *Page* 71
 3. Can scratch glass   *Page* 77
   a. Brass color   *Page* 77
   b. Reddish-brown color   *Page* 79
   c. Gray or black color   *Page* 80

B. Nonmetallic luster   *Page* 85
 1. Leaves colored mark on streak plate   *Page* 85
   a. Green or blue mineral color   *Page* 85
   b. Red or orange mineral color   *Page* 88
   c. Yellow mineral color   *Page* 91
   d. Brown mineral color   *Page* 93
 2. Leaves white mark or scratch on streak plate   *Page* 95
   a. Shows good cleavage   *Page* 95
    1. Can be scratched by fingernail   *Page* 95
    2. Cannot be scratched by fingernail, but can be scratched by copper coin   *Page* 99

COVELLITE

KEYS: Metallic luster. Can mark paper. Blue color.
Streak: Gray or black. Cleavage: I direction.
Specific Gravity: 4.6–4.8 (medium weight).

Indigo blue —▶

Turns purple
when wet —▶

Often iridescent
tarnish —▶

Cleaves into
thin flexible
plates ◀—

Named after N. Covelli (1790–1829), the man who discovered it on Mount Vesuvius, covellite is copper sulfide (CuS). It is not too common a mineral, but a number of good localities have been described, and it serves as a minor ore of copper. It is associated with other copper minerals, often in the richest part of the vein, and seems to have altered from them. Most covellite does not occur in crystals but rather in irregular pieces. Large crystals, singly and in groups, beautifully surfaced with an iridescent coating, have come from the Calabona mine at Alghero on the Mediterranean island of Sardinia. Similar specimens occur at Butte, Mont.—"the richest hill on earth"—where covellite is fairly abundant. It is found on Luzon Island in the Philippines and was formerly mined at Kennecott, Alaska, in large masses of the distinctive indigo-blue color that identifies this attractive metallic mineral. Several places in Colorado and a few in Wyoming and Utah have furnished some covellite. Argentina and other countries in South America also produce it. Bor, Yugoslavia, and Leogang, Austria, are among the chief European sources.

GALENA

KEYS: Metallic luster. Can mark paper. Gray or black color.
Streak: Lead-gray. Cleavage: 3 directions.
Specific Gravity: 7.4–7.6 (heavy).

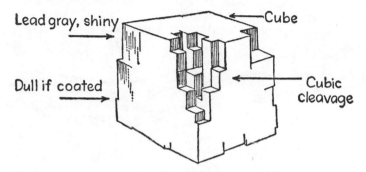

Lead gray, shiny ← Cube

Dull if coated ← Cubic cleavage

Galena is lead sulfide (PbS). It is by far the chief ore of lead, as well as an important ore of silver, which is present as a valuable "impurity." Silver is especially apt to be found by assaying the fine-grained variety known as steel galena, in which the right-angled cleavage that is so characteristic of the mineral may not be readily visible. Worldwide in distribution, galena is noteworthy in places as separated as Broken Hill, Australia; Freiberg and the Harz Mountains, Germany; the mining districts of Cornwall, Cumberland, and Derbyshire, England; and Leadville, Colo. In the United States galena can be found in metal-bearing veins and in limestone at many localities. It is particularly abundant in the Mississippi Valley from Wisconsin to Missouri, in the Tri-state area where Kansas, Oklahoma, and Missouri come together, and in the Rocky Mountain states of Idaho, Utah, and Colorado. The otherwise shiny surface of galena becomes dull when coated with a film of other substances; and, upon oxidizing, galena alters to anglesite and cerussite. Interesting combinations of galena with other minerals are often found in various rocks. Such an occurrence is the one at the Sullivan mine, Kimberley, B. C.

STIBNITE

KEYS: Metallic luster. Can mark paper. Gray or black color.
Streak: Lead-gray. **Cleavage:** I direction.
Specific Gravity: 4.6 (medium weight).

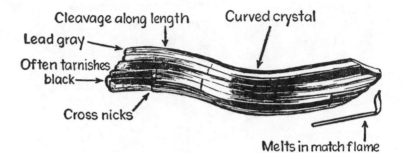

Cleavage along length   Curved crystal
Lead gray
Often tarnishes
black
Cross nicks
Melts in match flame

Antimony sulfide in chemical composition (Sb_2S_3), stibnite is the most important ore of antimony. From the extensive mines at Ichinokawa on the island of Shikoku, Japan, have come truly magnificent crystals, nearly 2 feet long and possessing many brilliant terminal faces. Groups of these are in the proud ownership of leading museums. An unusual feature of stibnite crystals is their curved or twisted appearance, as though they had been warped. The excellent crystals from Felsöbánya, Rumania, sometimes penetrate tabular specimens of barite. At Bau, in Borneo, large crystals are also found. Some well-crystallized material occurs near Hollister and elsewhere in California. Massive stibnite is produced in quantity in Hunan Province, China, where the world's largest deposits are situated. Stibnite is fusible enough to be melted in a match flame. White and yellow oxides of antimony often coat its surface, and stibnite loses its brightness when exposed to light. The dark powder was used by the ancients to blacken their eyebrows. Today stibnite enters directly into the manufacture of fireworks, vulcanized rubber, and medicines.

MOLYBDENITE

KEYS: Metallic luster. Can mark paper. Gray or black color.
Streak: Dark-gray, with greenish tinge.
Cleavage: 1 direction.
Specific Gravity: 4.6–4.7 (medium weight).

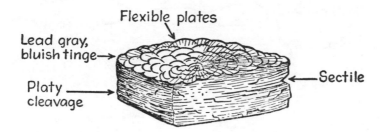

A sulfide of molybdenum (MoS_2) and the principal ore of that strategic industrial and military metal, molybdenite is so tricky to pronounce that miners simply call it "molly." Crisscrossed throughout with thin veins of it is Bartlett Mountain, rising behind Climax, Colo., to an altitude of 11,300 feet—the greatest concentration of molybdenite on this planet. For large crystals, however, the collector would have to go to such places as Bluehill Bay, Me.; Edison, N.J.; Renfrew County, Ont.; or as distant as Kingsgate, New South Wales. Thick sheets of the mineral have been taken from the very old rocks that underlie New York City. The resemblance between molybdenite and graphite is strong; perhaps the bluish tone to its color and the greenish tinge to its streak on porcelain will help you recognize molybdenite, and also it is heavier. Molybdenite is commonly found in granite and quartz, which are not the typical host rocks for graphite. The yellow dust on the top and in cracks is an alteration product, ferrimolybdite, which might easily be mistaken for sulfur or one of the secondary uranium minerals.

GRAPHITE

KEYS: Metallic luster. Can mark paper. Gray or black color.
Streak: Black. **Cleavage:** I direction.
Specific Gravity: 2.1–2.2 (light).

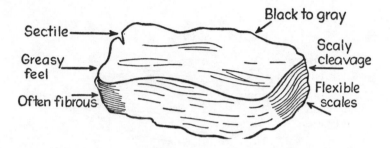

Sectile

Greasy feel

Often fibrous

Black to gray

Scaly cleavage

Flexible scales

Like diamond, graphite consists solely of crystallized carbon (C). The extraordinary difference between these two minerals in color, hardness, conductivity, and crystallization is the most remarkable contrast in all mineralogy. Whereas diamond is a nonconductor of electricity, graphite is a good conductor; whereas diamond crystals are common, graphite crystals are scarce and poorly developed. A curious fact is that graphite is really the more stable form of carbon, for diamond will change to it when heated. The greasy feel of graphite and the way it soils the fingers indicate its uses as a lubricant for machinery, a protective coating for metals, and the so-called lead for pencils. This last use, its original one, gave graphite its name, from the Greek word for "to write." Fine crystals come from Sterling Hill, N.J. The best-known occurrence in the United States is near the Revolutionary War fort of Ticonderoga, N.Y. Graphite is also found with coal in Rhode Island. Korea, however, has produced more commercial graphite in one year than any other country. A more consistent output comes from Madagascar, Ceylon, Mexico, Siberia, and Central Europe.

PYROLUSITE

Keys: Metallic luster. Can mark paper. Gray or black color.
Streak: Black. Cleavage: 2 directions.
Specific Gravity: 4.4–4.5 (medium weight).

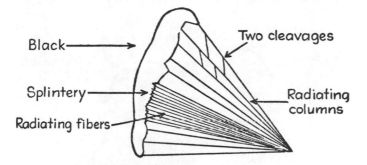

Black

Two cleavages

Splintery

Radiating
columns

Radiating fibers

An oxide of manganese (MnO_2) and the most abundant
ore of that metal, pyrolusite is a widespread mineral.
When in well-developed crystals, such as those of Horni
Blatna, Czechoslovakia, it is termed polianite, which is
very different from the common massive pyrolusite, being
hard enough then to scratch glass. Most frequently the
crystals are actually those of another manganese mineral
called manganite, which have changed chemically, losing
water but retaining their original shape. Pyrolusite is at
its charming best when it assumes fanciful scenic patterns
in chalcedony quartz, turning it into moss agate. Similar
plantlike designs are developed on slabs of sandstone and
limestone. Ordinary pyrolusite, on the contrary, which
is often soft enough to soil the hands a dirty black, is
scarcely attractive. Sometimes it takes on a characteristic
bluish cast. Usually pyrolusite is mixed with other manganese ores, all of them being mined together under the
name *wad*. The most extensive deposits are in the Soviet
Union, central India, Republic of South Africa, Ghana,
and Brazil. Pyrolusite acts as a decolorizing agent in glass
and is used in batteries.

61

GOLD

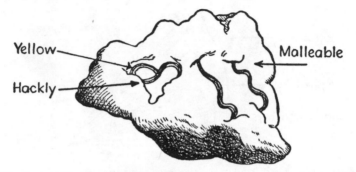

Yellow — Hackly — Malleable

Native gold (Au) is never found entirely pure. A varying proportion of silver is always present; when the percentage is high, the alloy is called electrum. Gold from Australia is noted for its low silver content. Well-developed crystals are extremely rare, making their appealing beauty all the more tantalizing. Exquisite, indeed, are the dendritic or fernlike groups. In public museums in Denver and nearby Golden, Colo., are displayed two vaults of wonderful specimens from that state. Gold ranges in size from the Welcome Stranger nugget found at Ballarat, Australia, which weighed 2,280 ounces, down to the "flour gold" in the Snake River, Ore., which requires about 5,000 of the minute particles to be worth one cent. Gold can be distinguished from the various kinds of "fool's gold"—pyrite, chalcopyrite, mica—by its heaviness and malleability. Since 1886 the South African district of Witwatersrand, familiarly called the Rand, has produced over 16,000 tons of gold valued at more than 12 billion dollars, from dozens of mines centering around Johannesburg. The ranking gold mine of the Western Hemisphere is the Homestake mine at Lead, S.D.

COPPER

KEYS: Metallic luster. Cannot mark paper, but can be scratched by knife blade. Copper color.

Fracture: Hackly. Specific Gravity: 8.9 (heavy).

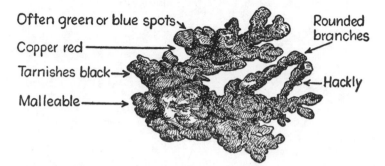

Often green or blue spots

Copper red

Tarnishes black→

Malleable

Rounded branches

←—Hackly

Native copper (Cu) was formerly the main source of copper, but various sulfide minerals now provide most of our needs for this indispensable metal. The native mineral is still a favorite of collectors, however, because of the interesting shapes it assumes. The stupendous deposits on the Keweenaw Peninsula in northern Michigan dwarf everything else of their kind in existence. Here, for more than a mile in depth, native copper, from great masses to tiny specks, has been mined. Branching skeletons, tiny scales, twisted wires, hollow shells shaped like human skulls, stream-worn pebbles—these are all typical of the Michigan copper. One enormous piece weighing 420 tons was found in 1857. Combinations of copper and native silver are called "half-breeds"; both minerals soon become tarnished and look alike, but when cleaned they stand in striking contrast to each other. Another Michigan occurrence consists of copper enclosed in transparent calcite; unaffected by tarnish, the copper gleams in its pristine state like gold. Native copper is also found at Corocoro, Bolivia, and in small amounts in other countries. The island of Cyprus, an early source of copper, gave its name to it.

MILLERITE

KEYS: Metallic luster. Cannot mark paper, but can be scratched by knife blade. Copper color.

Streak: Greenish-black. Cleavage: 3 directions.

Specific Gravity: 5.3–5.7 (medium weight).

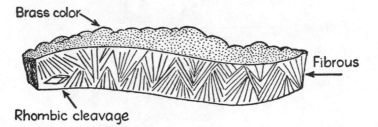

Brass color

Fibrous

Rhombic cleavage

Millerite, a subordinate nickel ore, is a sulfide of nickel (NiS). The German mineralogist Abraham Gottlob Werner first described millerite in 1789 and called it Haarkies. Given its present name for William Hallowes Miller, an English mineralogist (1801-1880), it is unusual among metallic minerals in consisting of slender brassy crystals which are often matted together like a wad of hair. Crystals of capillary texture occur in Wales at Merthyr Tydfil. Delicately tangled tufts are found in the crystal-lined rocks, known as geodes, which can be collected at Milwaukee, Wis.; St. Louis, Mo.; and Keokuk, Iowa. Velvety coatings of millerite come from the Gap mine in Lancaster County, Pa. Various localities in Germany yield needles of millerite. Interesting occurrences of millerite include sublimates from volcanic fumes at Mount Vesuvius, coal beds in the Saar, and the 25-ton Santa Catharina (Brazil) meteorite. Millerite is never found in large quantities. It is generally formed at low temperatures and may alter from other nickel minerals. The bright-scarlet chemical test for nickel will distinguish closely fibrous millerite from fibrous marcasite.

64

CHALCOPYRITE

KEYS: Metallic luster. Cannot mark paper, but can be scratched by knife blade. Copper color.

Streak: Greenish-black. Fracture: Uneven.

Specific Gravity: 4.1–4.3 (medium weight).

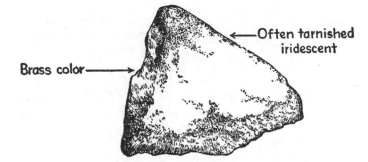

Brass color———→

←———Often tarnished iridescent

A copper–iron sulfide ($CuFeS_2$), chalcopyrite was so named in 1725 to distinguish it from regular pyrite, which does not contain copper except as an impurity. Like pyrite, it is one of the minerals referred to as fool's gold, and its brassy color resembles gold more than that of pyrite does. Chalcopyrite may also tarnish to give an iridescent appearance. Unlike pyrite it can be scratched by a knife, and unlike true gold it is brittle. It is not only the most common of all copper minerals, but it also frequently carries valuable amounts of gold or silver. It is associated with nickel deposits in a number of places. Rich pieces occur in the Noranda gold mine in the Rouyn district of Quebec. The mines at Ducktown, Tenn., should be mentioned for the quality of their chalcopyrite. Large perfect and sharp crystals have been obtained at Ellenville, N.Y., and in Chester County, Pa. A curious massive type, found in some mines in Cornwall, England, has a rounded surface and is known as blistered copper ore. Distributed throughout a huge ore body at Rio Tinto, Spain, chalcopyrite has long been mined there for copper and gold.

NICCOLITE

KEYS: Metallic luster. Cannot mark paper, but can be scratched by knife blade. Copper color.

Streak: Brownish-black. **Fracture:** Uneven.

Specific Gravity: 7.8 (heavy).

Pinkish copper color →

Often green ←coating

←Columnar structure

A nickel arsenide (NiAs), niccolite is unusually attractive for a metallic mineral. Many times called copper nickel by miners because of its coppery color and nickel content, it is one of the lesser ores of nickel. As early as 1694 it was known in Germany as *Kupfernickel,* and from this name was taken our word for the white metal. Concentric shells a foot in diameter, alternating with zones of arsenopyrite, come from Natsume, Japan. Crystals are exceedingly rare, a few having been found at Richelsdorf and Eisleben, Germany. The typical occurrence of niccolite is with silver, cobalt, and other nickel ores. These associations are important in Germany, Czechoslovakia, and Canada. In the United States some niccolite has been reported from New Jersey and Colorado. A thin green crust of annabergite often covers specimens of niccolite and may be a useful clue for determining the presence of niccolite beneath the ground. The reddish tinge of niccolite is different from the color of any of the other minerals described in this book, though it is similar to that of certain copper arsenides, and so a test for nickel might be necessary.

66

PYRRHOTITE

KEYS: Metallic luster. Cannot mark paper, but can be scratched by knife blade. Copper color.

Streak: Dark grayish-black. Fracture: Uneven.

Specific Gravity: 4.6 (medium weight).

Granular texture →

←Bronze color

Often tarnished ←dark brown

←Magnetic

Pyrrhotite is iron sulfide (FeS), with always a slight deficiency of iron that puzzled mineralogists for a long while. It has been called magnetic pyrite because it somewhat resembles pyrite and it is the only common mineral except magnetite to be noticeably magnetic. Thick crystals have been collected at the Morro Velho gold mine in Brazil. Smaller but good crystals have come from Kongsberg, Norway, and Andreasberg, Germany. Large crystal groups are known at Loben, Austria, and elsewhere in Central Europe. Great amounts of massive material are mined at Sudbury, Ont., where they are intimately mixed with pentlandite, a nickel sulfide that resembles pyrrhotite but is not magnetic. Ducktown, Tenn., is an important locality for ordinary pyrrhotite. The Western states yield this mineral in a moderate quantity. The word pyrrhotite, with its so difficult spelling, means reddish. The variety called troilite has been known in meteorites since 1766 and comes close to being pure iron sulfide. Troilite of terrestrial origin has been found in Del Norte County, Calif.

BORNITE

KEYS: Metallic luster. Cannot mark paper, but can be scratched by knife blade. Purple color.

Streak: Gray-black. Fracture: Uneven.

Specific Gravity: 5.1 (medium weight).

Bronze color ——→

←—Purple tarnish

This copper–iron sulfide (Cu_5FeS_4) is a significant ore of copper. Although bornite is a common enough mineral, crystals of it are rare, and so only irregular masses are usually found. Even these pieces, which should be readily recognized by their brownish-bronzy color on a freshly fractured surface, are disguised by the purplish tarnish which steals over them, covering them with a bright iridescence and giving bornite the miners' names of pea-cock ore, purple copper ore, and horseflesh ore. Any specimen suspected of being bornite should be broken open to expose a new area for observation, to see if the tarnish gives way to a bronze hue. The color of the bornite from Androka, Madagascar, is very choice. Large amounts of bornite are mined in a number of countries of Latin America and at Butte, Mont. It is also important at Mt. Lyell, Tasmania. The rare crystals used to be found in the United States at Bristol, Conn. This mineral was named in 1832 after Ignaz von Born, an eminent Austrian mineralogist who lived from 1742 to 1791.

CUPRITE

KEYS: Metallic luster. Cannot mark paper, but can be scratched by knife blade. Red or brown color.

Streak: Brownish-red. Fracture: Uneven.
Specific Gravity: 6.0 (medium weight).

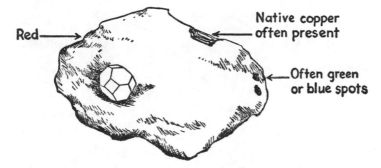

Copper oxide (Cu_2O) in composition, cuprite is an ore of copper; its name refers to this metal. The crystal forms of cuprite are highly interesting to the mineral collector. The most fascinating of the forms consists of a brilliant red mat of hairlike crystals, drawn out to needle length; this variety is called chalcotrichite (meaning "hair copper") and is much in demand for its exceptional beauty. The best specimens come from Morenci, Ariz., and from old copper mines near Gwennap, England. Fine crystals of the usual types of cuprite occur in several mines in Cornwall, England, and even larger ones come from Chessy, France. The name ruby copper suggests the appearance of the more desirable specimens. At Gumeschevsk in the Ural Mountains pieces of cuprite are perforated by cavities lined with later crystals of the same mineral. Cuprite is an important source of copper at Bisbee, Ariz. It is associated with other copper minerals, and some native copper is almost always present and aids in its identification. Ancient bronze and copper objects of art show tiny crystals of cuprite which have grown upon them during the passage of centuries.

69

GOETHITE

KEYS: Metallic luster. Cannot mark paper, but can be scratched by knife blade. Red or brown color.

Streak: Brownish-yellow. Cleavage: I direction.

Specific Gravity: 3.3–4.3 (medium weight).

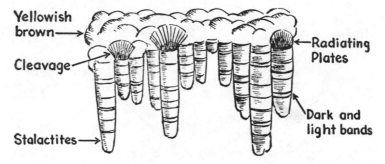

Yellowish brown → Radiating Plates

Cleavage

Dark and light bands

Stalactites →

Iron hydroxide with the chemical formula $HFeO_2$ was named goethite after the German poet and philosopher Johann Wolfgang von Goethe (1749-1832), who was a student and collector of minerals. It has undergone the strange experience of a mineral which was one day believed to be an uncommon one and almost the next day was learned to be one of the most abundant minerals. This odd development was the result of X-ray examinations which revealed that most of the iron ore that had always been known as limonite was actually crystalline in its atomic structure and therefore should really be called goethite instead. Fine crystallized specimens are found in cavities in granite in the Pikes Peak region of Colorado. The large cubes of goethite found at Pelican Point on the shore of Great Salt Lake, Utah, were originally pyrite and have changed chemically. Lostwithiel, England, is a classic locality for splendid crystals of goethite. This mineral is the main constituent of the important iron ores of Alsace-Lorraine, and it is widely distributed in Cuba. Goethite is found among the other iron minerals of the Lake Superior deposits, especially at Negaunee, Mich.

SILVER

KEYS: Metallic luster. Cannot mark paper, but can be scratched by knife blade. Gray or black color.

Streak: Silver-white. **Fracture:** Hackly.

Specific Gravity: 10.5 (very heavy).

When free of tarnish, silver (symbol, Ag) can be a handsome mineral. With its fernlike designs, network patterns, and crystal groups it resembles copper and gold except in color. Wire silver and crystals of unsurpassed beauty were produced for hundreds of years at Kongsberg, Norway, some of the masses weighing as much as 750 pounds. At Freiberg and Schneeberg, Germany, are situated other silver mines of considerable age. Aspen, Colo., is famous for its twisted masses of wire silver, and for the largest silver nuggets ever found, one of which, weighing 1,840 pounds, was too large to be hauled from the Mollie Gibson mine in an ore bucket. The fabulous "silver sidewalk" of the La Rose mine at Cobalt, Ont., was a slab of almost solid metal 100 feet long and 60 feet thick. Another Canadian silver locality is in the pitchblende deposits at Great Bear Lake. The Coeur d'Alene district in Idaho is also a prominent place for native silver. Mexico is the world's leading producer of silver, which may well be regarded as a Western Hemisphere metal, even though known to prehistoric man on the other continents.

71

ENARGITE

KEYS: Metallic luster. Cannot mark paper, but can be scratched by knife blade. Gray or black color.

Streak: Grayish-black. Cleavage: 2 directions.

Specific Gravity: 4.4 (medium weight).

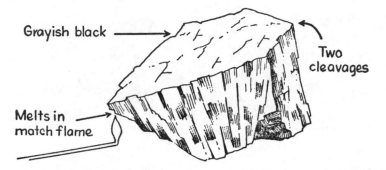

Grayish black

Two cleavages

Melts in match flame

A sulfide of copper and arsenic (Cu_3AsS_4) , enargite is an ore of copper, closely resembling stibnite except for its somewhat darker color—a test for copper is the easiest way to distinguish between them with certainty. Enargite is particularly important at Butte, Mont., where it also yields arsenic oxide ("white arsenic") for the chemical industry. The deposits in Utah at Bingham Canyon and Tintic also produce substantial amounts of enargite. California, Nevada, and Colorado furnish small quantities, especially the silver mines in the San Juan Mountains of Colorado. Outside of the United States the main sources of enargite are in South America, in the noted copper mines at Cerro de Pasco and Morococha, both in Peru, and at Chuquicamata, Chile. A large deposit exists at Bor, Yugoslavia, but otherwise enargite is not common in Europe. The name of this mineral comes from a Greek word meaning distinct, because of its definite cleavage, and was applied to it in 1850. As antimony replaces the arsenic, enargite grades into famatinite, which was named after the Sierra de Famatina, Argentina.

PYRARGYRITE

KEYS: Metallic luster. Cannot mark paper, but can be scratched by knife blade. Gray or black color.

Streak: Brownish-red. Cleavage: 3 directions.

Specific Gravity: 5.8 (medium weight).

Pyrargyrite, sulfide of silver and antimony (Ag_3SbS_3), is called dark-ruby silver because of its deep ruby-red color. As atoms of arsenic substitute for those of antimony, pyrargyrite grades into proustite, known as light-ruby silver. Except for the transparency and depth of color, these two minerals closely resemble each other, and the two together are called the ruby silvers. Choice crystals of either are clear and richly colored, like fine garnets or rubies. Most ore specimens, however, are gray until freshly broken, when the reddish hue appears on the newly revealed face like a blush. Pyrargyrite is the more abundant of these two minerals and is an important ore of silver, occurring in many mines in the Western states and South America. Exceptional crystals of pyrargyrite come from Andreasberg, Germany, and magnificent ones of proustite—among the most beautiful minerals known —from Chañarcillo, Chile. In 1865 an enormous mass of crystalline proustite weighing over 500 pounds was taken from the Poorman mine at Silver City, Idaho, which has also yielded substantial amounts of pyrargyrite.

PITCHBLENDE

KEYS: Metallic luster. Cannot mark paper, but can be scratched by knife blade. Gray or black color.
Streak: Brownish-black. **Fracture:** Uneven.
Specific Gravity: 6.5–8.5 (heavy).

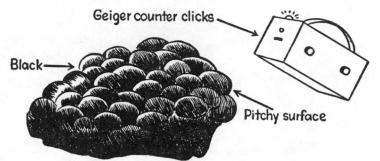

Geiger counter clicks

Black →

Pitchy surface

The principal material for the creation of atomic energy and the primary source of uranium, pitchblende is today without doubt the world's most strategic mineral. It is also one of the most historic of minerals, having been the original source of radium and the first substance in which helium (earlier detected in the sun) was discovered on the earth. Pitchblende is uranium oxide with a mixture of products caused by weathering and alteration. When the same mineral is of purer composition (dominantly UO_2) and occurs in crystals, it is called uraninite. The ratio between the uranium and the lead or helium formed by radioactive disintegration is a measure of the time that has elapsed since the mineral crystallized. The name pitchblende refers to the pitchy luster. The Katanga district of the Congo nation, and Great Bear Lake, Canada, are the main producers of pitchblende and uraninite. Older deposits of especial prominence are situated at Sankt Joachimsthal (now Jáchymov), Czechoslovakia, and Central City, Colo. Sparsely scattered crystals are collected at Grafton Center, N.H., and several places in Connecticut.

TETRAHEDRITE

KEYS: Metallic luster. Cannot mark paper, but can be scratched by knife blade. Gray or black color.

Streak: Black or brown. Fracture: Uneven.
Specific Gravity: 4.6–5.1 (medium weight).

Gray ⟶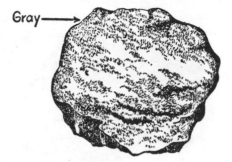

Tetrahedrite is a sulfide of copper, iron, and antimony [$(Cu,Fe)_{12}Sb_4S_{13}$], together with several other metals, of which silver is the most valuable. Hence it has a complex composition, and it serves as an ore of both copper and silver. First-rate crystals occur at Bingham, Utah; Bótes, Rumania; Ste.-Marie-aux-Mines, France; and Liskeard, England. The name of the mineral comes from the tetrahedral shape of the crystals—a wedge-shaped pyramid. Tetrahedrite is well distributed among the mining districts of Idaho, Utah, New Mexico, Nevada, Arizona, and California. Roman coins thrown into a hot spring at the French watering place of Bourbonne-les-Bains have been recovered with a natural incrustation of tetrahedrite. As the content of antimony decreases while that of arsenic increases, tetrahedrite grades into tennantite, named in honor of an English chemist, Smithson Tennant (1761-1815). Both minerals look alike; probably a good share of the Colorado specimens labeled tetrahedrite are actually the other member of this series. Definite and complex crystals of silver-bearing tennantite come from the Binnental, Switzerland.

75

CHALCOCITE

KEYS: Metallic luster. Cannot mark paper, but can be scratched by knife blade. Gray or black color.

Streak: Gray. Fracture: Conchoidal.

Specific Gravity: 5.5–5.8 (medium weight).

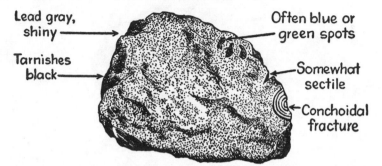

Lead gray, shiny

Tarnishes black

Often blue or green spots

Somewhat sectile

Conchoidal fracture

Chalcocite is copper sulfide (Cu_2S), one of the major ores of copper. In the type of deposit referred to as "porphyry copper" it occurs sparsely disseminated through the rock as a low-grade ore, which, however, can be extracted cheaply on a large scale. A zone spoken of as the "chalcocite blanket" is a feature of such deposits, which include Bingham in Utah and Ely in Nevada. Other important localities for chalcocite are Butte, Mont., and Kennecott, Alaska. Pure masses weighing tens of thousands of tons are common at Kennecott, where the most interesting occurrence is the "glacial ore," surrounded by ice. Large amounts of chalcocite also exist at Tsumeb, South-West Africa. Although scarce, choice crystals have come from Bristol, Conn., and mines in Cornwall, England. Somewhat sectile, chalcocite should not be confused with argentite, which can be cut much more readily. Like other copper minerals, chalcocite often has a thin coating of blue or green carbonate. Its shiny luster is seen only on fresh surfaces, which rather soon turn dull and black. The name comes from the Greek language and indicates brass or copper.

PYRITE

KEYS: Metallic luster. Can scratch glass. Brass color.
Streak: Greenish- to brownish-black. **Fracture:** Uneven.
Specific Gravity: 5.0–5.1 (medium weight).

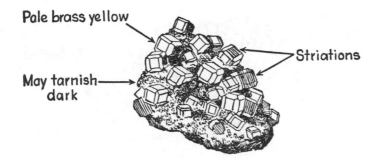

Pale brass yellow

Striations

May tarnish
dark

The most familiar form of iron sulfide (FeS_2) is pyrite. Its name alludes to the sparks that fly when it is struck with a hammer. More abundant than marcasite, which has the same chemical composition, it ranks as one of the commonest of minerals. Pyrite, in fact, is referred to as a persistent mineral because it occurs under almost every geologic condition. It is one of the minerals called fool's gold. Huge crystals of pyrite have come, among other places, from Leadville, Colo.; Ubina, Bolivia; and the island of Elba. The well-shaped crystals from Chester, Vt., are attractively embedded in a green rock. So-called iron-cross twins come from Schoharie, N.Y. At Sparta, Ill., are the "pyrite suns," which are radiating disks of the mineral. Of little value for its iron content, pyrite is often rich in gold and copper, as well as being a source of sulfur. Very large deposits occur at Rio Tinto, Spain, where they have been worked since the days of the Phoenicians. Some of the most interesting occurrences of pyrite are those in which it has replaced the organic matter of fossils; a few localities for such specimens are Holland Patent, N.Y., and Lyme Regis, England.

77

MARCASITE

KEYS: Metallic luster. Can scratch glass. Brass color.
Streak: Greenish-black. Fracture: Uneven.
Specific Gravity: 4.9 (medium weight).

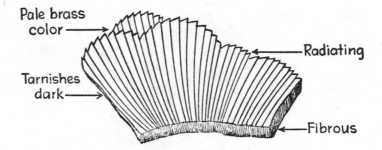

Pale brass color →

← Radiating

Tarnishes dark →

← Fibrous

Having exactly the same composition as pyrite, though not nearly so common, marcasite is iron sulfide (FeS_2). The curious spear and cockscomb forms of marcasite are actually twin crystals; at Dover, England, the spear-shaped specimens are believed locally to be relics of Roman weapons. Marcasite often grows as stalactites covered with pyramid-shaped crystals projecting outward like spikes on a war club. Rounded lumps of various sizes occur embedded in shale. In the former state of Württemberg, Germany, fossils from the age of dinosaurs are found to be replaced by marcasite. Leading localities for marcasite in the United States include Mineral Point, Wis., Galena, Ill., and the zinc and lead mines around Joplin, Mo. The name marcasite used to be applied to pyrite until a distinction was made between the two minerals, which have different atomic structures. Marcasite is much less apt than pyrite to be present as individual crystals, tending instead toward fibrous and radiating aggregates, especially in nodules. Because marcasite decomposes so readily, specimens fall to pieces quickly; unless they are kept in a dry atmosphere, they become covered with white powder.

HEMATITE

KEYS: Metallic luster. Can scratch glass. Reddish-brown color.

Streak: Reddish-brown. **Fracture:** Uneven.
Specific Gravity: 4.9–5.3 (medium weight).

Reddish brown

Surface often rounded

The word hematite, which refers to the iron oxide mineral having the formula Fe_2O_3, means bloodstone. It is certainly appropriate enough, on account of the Indian-red streak of this vital iron ore. There are several distinct varieties of hematite. When it occurs in crystals, it is black and shiny; Cumberland, England, and the island of Elba are the most noted sources for these handsome specimens, which are cut into intaglios (reverse cameos) for men's rings. Specimens that look like mica consist of small flakes which shine like mirrors—this kind is called specularite or specular hematite. So-called "iron roses," daintily curved like the petals of a flower, come from the St. Gotthard area, Switzerland. Rounded lumps are called kidney ore, and these are especially fine at Ulverston, England. Commercial deposits of hematite are of incredible extent in the Lake Superior region, along the Appalachian Mountains, in eastern Canada, and at Cerro Bolivar, Venezuela. Some of this material, called pencil ore, is fibrous; some of it, called oölitic hematite, consists of small rounded bits that resemble fish roe.

MAGNETITE

KEYS: Metallic luster. Can scratch glass. Gray or black color.

Streak: Black. Fracture: Even.

Specific Gravity: 5.2 (medium weight).

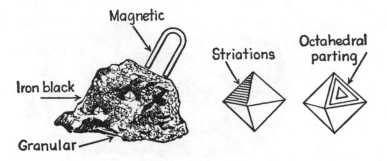

Owing to its strong magnetism this iron oxide mineral (Fe_3O_4) has been known since early times. Not only will a magnet pick up pieces of it quickly, but some specimens act as natural magnets themselves—these are called lodestone. An old story names magnetite after a shepherd, Magnes, whose shoes and staff were held to the ground by the attraction of lodestone for the iron nails in them. Powerful lodestone, exhibiting a north and a south pole, is found in the Ural, Altai, and Harz Mountains and on Elba. It also occurs, together with crystals of magnetite, at Magnet Cove, Ark. Other localities for excellent crystals are at Nordmark, Sweden; Arendal, Norway; Greiner, Austria; Scalotta, Italy; Vascau, Rumania; and Fiormeza, Cuba. Magnetite is the richest and one of the most abundant ores of iron, for which it is mined on a vast scale in Sweden, the Adirondack Mountains in New York, and the so-called Bushveld Complex in South Africa. Most of the black sand seen on ocean beaches, shifted into streaks by the waves and currents, is composed of magnetite grains washed out of rocks in the interior of the continent.

WOLFRAMITE

KEYS: Metallic luster. Can scratch glass. Gray or black color.

Streak: Brown or black. Cleavage: I direction.

Specific Gravity: 7.1–7.5 (heavy).

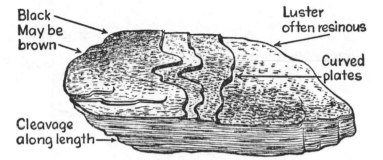

Black May be brown — Luster often resinous — Curved plates — Cleavage along length

An iron–manganese tungstate [$(Fe,Mn) WO_4$], wolframite is the most important ore of tungsten or wolfram, furnishing half of the world's supply from deposits in China. The richest source of all is in the Nan Ling Range in the southern part of China. Large reserves are also known in Burma, Malaya, Australia, and Bolivia. Fine crystals come from Czechoslovakia, Germany, and England. Other good localities for wolframite are in Portugal, Spain, the Transvaal, and Siberia. Wolframite is often associated with cassiterite, the chief ore of tin. In the United States it has been found to some extent in Arizona and the Black Hills of South Dakota. Wolframite has had different names in several languages, each derived from the same odd Latin name "wolf froth," the meaning of which is quite obscure. With a reduction in its proportion of iron, wolframite grades into huebnerite, which is very similar in appearance though browner, and less common. In the other direction, as the manganese decreases, wolframite grades into ferberite, a rather different-looking mineral, which is found in brilliant clusters of small black crystals in Boulder County, Colo.

ARSENOPYRITE

KEYS: Metallic luster. Can scratch glass. Gray or black color.

Streak: Black. Fracture: Uneven.
Specific Gravity: 5.9–6.2 (medium weight).

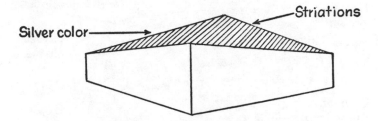

The most common arsenic mineral, arsenopyrite is an arsenide–sulfide of iron (FeAsS). Before it was given its present name in 1847 it was known by the peculiar name of mispickel. Large crystals from Tavistock, England, are noteworthy. The fine crystals at Franconia, N.H., are also familiar to collectors. Rounded masses as much as 1 foot in diameter, having alternating shells of niccolite, come from Natsume, Japan. At Deloro, Ont., arsenopyrite contains enough gold to make it valuable for that metal alone. Cobalt and silver are other metals that have been recovered from arsenopyrite. Thousands of other mining districts throughout the world yield specimens of arseno-pyrite, which is one of the first minerals to form. In the Tres Hermanes Mountains of New Mexico the crystals have grown as twins, in the shape of crosses and stars. Some of the crystal groups look like marcasite, from which they can usually be distinguished by their silvery-gray color, unless they have tarnished somewhat yellow; moreover, unlike marcasite, arsenopyrite never has a fibrous structure. It seems to have a harsh appearance.

CHROMITE

KEYS: Metallic luster. Can scratch glass. Gray or black color.

Streak: Dark-brown. Fracture: Uneven.

Specific Gravity: 4.6 (medium weight).

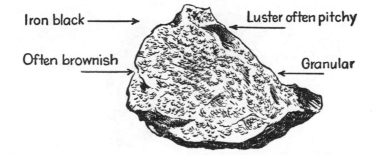

Iron black ⟶

Luster often pitchy ⟵

Often brownish ⟶

Granular ⟵

In composition an iron chromite ($FeCr_2O_4$) and in use the only ore of chromium, this mineral has an easy name to remember. Good crystals, which resemble those of magnetite and franklinite, are small and scarce; they are found, for instance, on the northern islands of Unst and Fetlar in the Shetland Islands. Chromite may be slightly magnetic but not enough to be mistaken for magnetite. A pitchy luster and a brownish cast to the color, while not necessarily present, are frequent enough to aid in recognizing chromite when you see it. Though hardly to be called a North American mineral, some of it has been mined along both coasts from Alaska to California and from Newfoundland to North Carolina. Meteorites sometimes contain chromite, which is typically a high-temperature mineral. Bricks made from it are so heat-resistant that they are used to line the walls of furnaces in which metals are melted. Chromite is extremely tough and hard to break, and it is more than durable enough to become a constituent of placer gravels, especially those that contain platinum, for the two minerals are formed and preserved under similar conditions.

ILMENITE

KEYS: Metallic luster. Can scratch glass. Gray or black color.

Streak: Black or brownish-red. **Fracture.** Even.

Specific Gravity: 4.7 (medium weight).

Iron black ⟶ 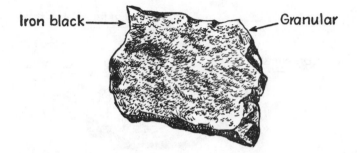 ⟵ Granular

An iron titanate ($FeTiO_3$), ilmenite was named after the Ilmen Mountains, Russia, the original locality. It has come a long way from being an undesirable impurity in iron ore to its present status as one of the most promising industrial minerals of our time. The enormous new deposit at Allard Lake, Que., contains enough ilmenite to supply the whole world. Interestingly, this very black mineral makes the whitest of all paints and the white smoke used for skywriting and smoke screens. Crystals of ilmenite that are bright or well-shaped are rare; they may look like dark hematite. Some occur in Orange County, N.Y., and crystals weighing over 16 pounds have been found at Kragerö, Norway. Crystals are also found at Chester, Mass., and at St. Christophe, France. The black sand of certain beaches contains large amounts of ilmenite; for example, at Pablo Beach, Florida, and on the extraordinary beaches, one of which extends for 15 miles, in Travancore, India. Massive ilmenite resembles magnetite but is nonmagnetic, although the two minerals are often intergrown so that they must be separated magnetically before they can be used.

MALACHITE

KEYS: Nonmetallic luster. Leaves colored mark on streak plate. Green or blue mineral color.

Hardness: $3\frac{1}{2}$–4. Fracture: Conchoidal.

Specific Gravity: 3.9–4.1 (heavy).

Green → Vitreous luster

Conchoidal fracture

Often velvety

Banded

Pale green streak

Malachite is a basic copper carbonate [$Cu_2(OH)_2(CO_3)$], and fizzes when touched by acid. Over one-half million pounds of the choice green mineral were taken from one pure mass of malachite in the Demidoff copper mine at Nizhni Tagil, in the Ural Mountains of Siberia. It was extensively used in Czarist Russia for table tops and other ornamental purposes. Another form of Russian malachite occurs in fibrous nodules having a silky luster; these were carved into exquisitely fashioned objects of art. The best crystals are found at Betzdorf, Germany, and the finest of those that have changed over from blue azurite come from Tsumeb, South-West Africa. The largest deposit of malachite is in the Katanga district of the Congo nation and Northern Rhodesia, where valuable copper ore is mined, as well as superb pieces of banded malachite well suited to being cut and polished. New Mexico and Arizona are the main producing states in the United States, although malachite can be found in the upper levels of almost every copper mine in the West. The green patina that appears on copper and bronze is in reality a thin tarnish of malachite.

AZURITE

KEYS: Nonmetallic luster. Leaves colored mark on streak plate. Green or blue mineral color.

Hardness: $3\frac{1}{2}$–4. Fracture: Conchoidal.

Specific Gravity: 3.7–3.8 (heavy).

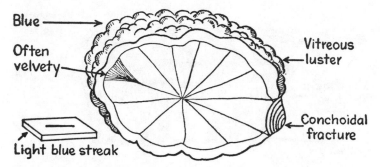

Blue

Often velvety

Light blue streak

Vitreous luster

Conchoidal fracture

Azurite, like malachite, is a basic copper carbonate $[Cu_3(OH)_2(CO_3)_2]$. It fizzes similarly in contact with acid. Its rich blue color, from which it receives its name, is as distinctive as the equally deep green of malachite; the two minerals often occur together in a wonderfully appealing combination of contrasting colors. Inasmuch as azurite readily changes to malachite, the result may be a crystal which retains the original shape of the azurite but which now has the green color and all the other properties of malachite. The perfect and lustrous crystals of azurite from Chessy, France, are the finest ever known, though Tsumeb, South-West Africa, has more recently become the chief locality for crystals of remarkable size and beauty. Arizona is the leading American state, but unfortunately most of the Bisbee copper mines that produced splendid crystals, singly and in groups, have now been deepened below the zone in which azurite exists. During the fifteenth and sixteenth centuries azurite was the most popular blue pigment among European painters, and it had been employed for the ancient wall paintings of the Orient.

CHRYSOCOLLA

KEYS: Nonmetallic luster. Leaves colored mark on streak plate. Green or blue mineral color.

Hardness: 2–4. Fracture: Conchoidal.

Specific Gravity: 2.0–2.2 (light).

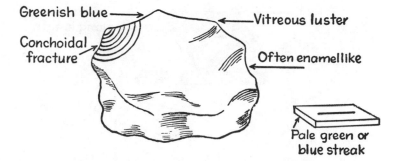

Greenish blue → Vitreous luster

Conchoidal fracture

Often enamellike

Pale green or blue streak

A hydrous copper silicate of indefinite composition [$(CuSiO_3.nH_2O)$], chrysocolla is a minor ore of copper. It is used as an ornamental stone, substituting for turquoise, which likewise varies between greenish and bluish hues. Although softer and not so well known or so valuable as turquoise, it is in some ways more durable because its delicate color is permanent, and the shining enamel-like surface which it often shows is quite attractive. Chrysocolla occurs in the upper part of copper mines, associated with other colorful minerals containing that metal. Excellent specimens come from various localities in Arizona, New Mexico, Chile, England, and the Belgian Congo. The only crystals that have ever been found were from Mackay, Idaho, and are of microscopic size. The word chrysocolla, meaning "gold glue," was given to a similar-looking mineral used in olden times to solder gold, and it was later transferred in error to this mineral. When impure, as it often is because of its somewhat variable content of water, chrysocolla becomes brown or black and has then been called pitchy copper ore.

87

RUTILE

KEYS: Nonmetallic luster. Leaves colored mark on streak plate. Red or orange mineral color.

Hardness: 6–6½. Fracture: Uneven.
Specific Gravity: 4.2–4.3 (heavy).

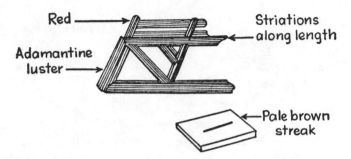

Red — Striations along length

Adamantine luster —

Pale brown streak

Rutile is the most familiar of the three minerals that are composed of titanium oxide and share the same formula (TiO_2), the others being anatase and brookite. The name rutile is derived from the Latin word for red, in reference to the color. The splendid specimens from Graves Mountain, Ga., are the finest in the United States. They consist of twinned crystals which repeat themselves until they make a complete ring. Magnet Cove, Ark., Stony Point, N.C., and Laws, Calif., are other outstanding American localities. Well-crystallized rutile comes from veins and rock crevices in a number of places in the Alps. Dark rutile crystals look a good deal like those of cassiterite, but they are not so heavy. Rolled pebbles are found in the diamond-bearing gravels in Brazil, and commercial deposits, where rutile is obtained as an ore of titanium, are found in the sand on Florida beaches. Needlelike red crystals of rutile are common as inclusions in quartz, which is then known as rutilated quartz; sagenite, a favorite of mineral collectors, is a related quartz material named from the network of crystals buried within it.

CINNABAR

KEYS: Nonmetallic luster. Leaves colored mark on streak plate. Red or orange mineral color.
Hardness: 2–2½. Fracture: Uneven.
Specific Gravity: 8.0–8.2 (very heavy).

Adamantine luster →

Red →

Scarlet streak

The chief ore of mercury (quicksilver) is cinnabar, mercury sulfide (HgS). Low-grade deposits are often deceiving because a thin crust of the bright red mineral gives a false appearance of richness. Impure cinnabar may be dark-red, almost black. Cinnabar forms near hot springs and is found near the earth's surface in areas of recent volcanic rocks. The most extensive occurrence in the world is at Almadén, Spain. Another large one is at Idria, Italy. Named after these ancient localities are the important California mines at New Almaden and New Idria. The mercury produced at New Almaden is credited with having made possible the tremendous gold production that took place during the California gold rush of the years immediately after 1848. At Terlingua, Tex., some of the cinnabar has altered to a group of rare mercury minerals. Pebbles of cinnabar, rolled round by stream action, are panned in gold placers in Dutch Guiana. Large crystals are obtained in China, and excellent ones also come from near Belgrade, Yugoslavia, and in Pike County, Ark. These show a pronounced cleavage not obvious in the usual finely granular material.

REALGAR

KEYS: Nonmetallic luster. Leaves colored mark on streak plate. Red or orange mineral color.
Hardness: $1\frac{1}{2}$–2. Cleavage: 1 direction.
Specific Gravity: 3.5 (medium weight).

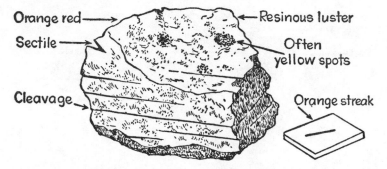

Orange red → ← Resinous luster
Sectile → Often yellow spots
Cleavage → Orange streak

Realgar is arsenic sulfide (AsS) in its simplest form. It is not too stable a mineral, and exposure to light, which should be avoided, causes it to change rapidly from red to orange, eventually becoming yellow orpiment. The two minerals are almost always found together in nature. Besides ore veins, hot springs and volcanoes are the chief sources of realgar. Good crystals, otherwise rare, come from Mercur, Utah; the Binnental, Switzerland; and the island of Corsica in the Mediterranean. Fine specimens of this attractive mineral are also found at Manhattan, in Nevada. In Rumania it occurs with ores of silver and lead, occasionally in lovely translucent crystals. Nests of realgar are sometimes clustered in beds of clay. Thin coatings of realgar are deposited around Yellowstone geysers (in the Norris geyser basin) and Italian steam vents. The curious word realgar is derived from an Arabic term, *rahj al-ghār,* meaning "powder of the mine." The natural mineral was formerly used as a pigment and in fireworks, but is no longer. Realgar is softer and lighter in weight than cinnabar, which it may superficially appear to be.

ORPIMENT

KEYS: Nonmetallic luster. Leaves colored mark on streak plate. Yellow mineral color.

Hardness: $1\frac{1}{2}$–2. Cleavage: 1 direction.

Specific Gravity: 3.5 (medium weight).

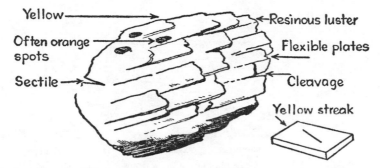

Yellow — Resinous luster
Often orange spots — Flexible plates
Sectile — Cleavage
Yellow streak

Orpiment, like realgar, is arsenic sulfide but has a different formula (As_2S_3). Its tabular crystals are very uncommon and almost always small. Those from Mercur, Utah, however, are exceptionally large and fine; excellent ones also have come from Balin, Russia. Substantial amounts of orpiment occur at Acobambilla in Peru, and Julamerk in Turkey. The hot water at Steamboat Springs, Nev.; Yellowstone National Park, Wyo.; and Shimotsuke, Japan, deposits orpiment from springs and geysers onto the surrounding rocks, as do smoke vents in Italy. Lemon-yellow orpiment is often seen as an alteration product on pieces of realgar, and it is frequently scattered through certain layered rocks. At some places it has resulted from fires in a mine. Its name comes from the Latin name which means "golden paint," in reference to its color and because it was believed to contain gold—a compliment, indeed, to its vivid color. A little natural orpiment is used as a dye and in tanning skins, but the main use of the mineral is as specimens for collections. The handsome combinations of orpiment and realgar add life to any display.

CARNOTITE

KEYS: Nonmetallic luster. Leaves colored mark on streak plate. Yellow mineral color.

Hardness: 1–2. Fracture: Earthy.
Specific Gravity: 5.0 (heavy).

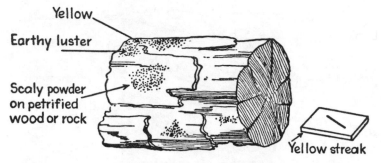

Yellow

Earthy luster

Scaly powder
on petrified
wood or rock

Yellow streak

Carnotite is a complex mineral containing uranium, vanadium, and radium. Its chemical formula is close to $K_2(UO_2)_2(VO_4)_2 \cdot 3H_2O$. All three of the metals mentioned have in the past been extracted from it on a commercial scale. First discovered in Colorado, it was taken to France for analysis and was named there after a French mining engineer and chemist, Marie-Adolphe Carnot (1839-1920). It and pitchblende are significant ores of uranium in the United States, and this is now its sole use. In the remote plateau country of the Four Corners region—the only place in the nation where four states come together (Colorado, Utah, Arizona, New Mexico) —carnotite occurs uniquely in sandstone, associated with dinosaur bones, petrified wood, and vegetable matter. Two petrified logs from Calamity Gulch, Colo., and the rock between them yielded $350,000 in the three valuable metals. A little carnotite is known in other states, including Pennsylvania, and it forms a thin film on rock at Radium Hill, South Australia. Tiny micalike crystals can be expected at times, but a powdery or loosely granular form is the usual aspect.

SPHALERITE

KEYS: Nonmetallic luster. Leaves colored mark on streak plate. Brown mineral color.

Hardness: 3.5–4.0. Cleavage: 6 directions.

Specific Gravity: 3.9–4.2 (heavy).

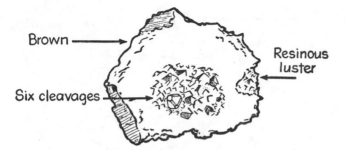

Brown — Resinous luster — Six cleavages

Zinc sulfide (ZnS), sphalerite, is the principal ore of zinc. Because it assumes various appearances, sphalerite is sometimes difficult to recognize and may be mistaken for minerals that bring a higher price; from this risk of disappointment it has obtained its name, which means treacherous. The name preferred in England is blende, which has a similar significance. Miners use additional terms, including zinc blende, blackjack, ruby zinc, and still others. Pure sphalerite is colorless, but iron is nearly always present, giving it a color that ranges from yellow to brown to black and may even be green. The world's greatest deposit of sphalerite is in the Tri-state area where Missouri, Kansas, and Oklahoma come together; the specimens from here are numerous and attractive. Some are as radiant as rubies. Butte, Mont., has also furnished remarkably good specimens. Fine groups occur at Alston Moor, England, and other localities in that country. Large masses of gorgeous golden color occur at Picos de Europa, Spain, and Cananea, Mexico. Unusually pure sphalerite has been analyzed from the Prince Frederick mine in Arkansas.

CASSITERITE

KEYS: Nonmetallic luster. Leaves colored mark on streak plate. Brown mineral color.

Hardness: 6–7. Fracture: Uneven.

Specific Gravity: 7.0 (very heavy).

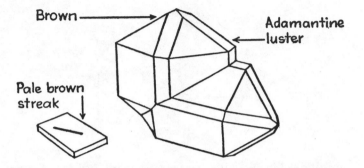

Brown ⟶ Adamantine luster

Pale brown streak

The oxide of tin, cassiterite (SnO_2), is the most important ore of tin. The vast deposits which stretch for 1,000 miles from Burma and China to the republics of Malaya and Indonesia yield cassiterite in large amounts, and it is also mined in Bolivia, Nigeria, the Congo, Australia, and a few other countries. Great Britain, known to ancient geographers as the Cassiterides or Tin Islands, was long a significant producer. Perhaps the most unusual occurrence of this mineral are the deerhorns found to have changed to cassiterite in the streams of Cornwall, England. Odd shapes exist, including sparable tin (like a cobbler's nail), wood tin (resembling a piece of dried wood), and toad's-eye tin. Because they are so often found in placer deposits, pebbles of cassiterite are popularly known as stream tin. Perfect crystals come from the tin mines of both the German and Czech sides of the mountain range called the Erzgebirge. Cassiterite is uncommon in the United States, marking a serious mineral deficiency, though it is found in a dozen scattered states, especially in the Black Hills of South Dakota.

MICA

KEYS: Nonmetallic luster. Leaves white mark or scratch on streak plate. Shows good cleavage. Can be scratched by fingernail.

Color: White, green = **muscovite**. Black, dark-brown = **biotite**. Yellowish-brown = **phlogopite**. Pink, purple = **lepidolite**.

Specific Gravity: 2.7–3.3 (medium weight, but may float on water because flaky).

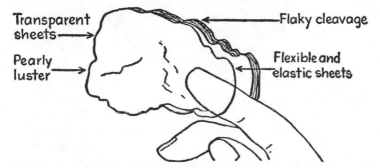

Transparent sheets →

Pearly luster →

← Flaky cleavage

← Flexible and elastic sheets

Mica is a group of minerals which are potassium-aluminum silicates and give off water when heated. They all have the remarkable property of peeling into thin sheets which not only can be bent but are also elastic, springing back to their original position when released, unless they have been carelessly broken. Thick crystals are called books, as they resemble a volume having many leaves or pages. The several kinds of mica have different colors because of variations in the chemical formula. Muscovite, also called white mica, has the simplest composition. Crystals of muscovite 33 feet long have been found in Ontario. The replacement of aluminum by magnesium produces phlogopite or brown mica; when both magnesium and iron are present, the mineral is biotite or black mica. Lepidolite or lithia mica has a lovely pink or purple color. White or light-brown mica, familiar as isinglass, is a strategic mineral for insulation.

CHLORITE

KEYS: Nonmetallic luster. Leaves white mark or scratch on streak plate. Shows good cleavage. Can be scratched by fingernail.

Color: Green. Specific Gravity: 2.6–3.0 (medium weight).

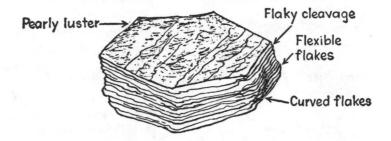

Pearly luster — Flaky cleavage — Flexible flakes — Curved flakes

Chlorite is a group of hydrous silicate minerals which resemble green mica except that they are not elastic. Their curved leaves can be bent but do not return to the original position, as do the flat flakes of true mica. They seem to have a slightly soapy feel. The individual members of this group go under such names as clinochlore, penninite, and prochlorite; it is usually not necessary to try to distinguish among them. Their chemical formulas, as is the case with so many of the silicate minerals, are very complex. Chlorite makes up the mass of certain widespread green rocks and frequently dusts the surface of other minerals or occurs inside them. At Zermatt in the Swiss Alps are large green crystals of chlorite, which are especially noted among mineral collectors. Substantial plates are found at West Chester, Pa. Garnet is one of a number of minerals which occur in chlorite and alter to it; many of the big crystals from near Salida, Colo., have "rotted" to chlorite almost all the way through. The word chlorite means green, and this mineral is responsible for the color of many rocks, as a result of weathering and the action of hot water.

Minerals in Color

The following pages contain illustrations of forty-six minerals in full color. Arranged in alphabetical order for easy reference, they will be a further aid in identifying some of the minerals that are described in the text. All of these colored illustrations are reproduced by courtesy of Ward's Natural Science Establishment, Inc., Rochester, New York. They are from Ward's Color Slides for Mineralogy (photographs by Katherine H. Jensen), and from the Harvard Mineral Collection.

AMBER
Baltic.

ANDALUSITE
Variety Chiastolite.
Madera County, California.

APATITE
Auburn, Maine.

AURICHALCITE
Kelly, New Mexico.

BERYL
Variety Aquamarine, Klein
Spitzkopje, South-West Africa.

AZURITE
Bisbee, Arizona.

BARITE
Felsöbanya, Rumania.

CALCITE
Egremont, Cumberland,
England.

CHALCOPYRITE
St. Agnes, Cornwall, England.

CINNABAR
Mercur, Utah.

COPPER
Houghton County, Michigan.

CROCOITE
Near Dundas, Tasmania.

CUPRITE
Variety Chalcotrichite,
Bisbee, Arizona.

DATOLITE
Houghton County, Michigan.

DIAMOND
Kimberley, South Africa.

FLUORITE
Cave-in-Rock, Illinois.

FRANKLINITE
Franklin, New Jersey.

GOETHITE
Ishpeming, Michigan.

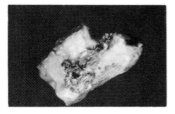

GOLD
Cederberg Mine,
El Dorado County, California.

GYPSUM
Variety Selenite,
Elsworth, Ohio.

CARNOTITE
San Juan County, Colorado.

HALITE
Wieliczka, Galicia.

HEMATITE
Minas Gerais, Brazil.

IRON METEORITES
Henbury, Australia.

LIMONITE
Berks County, Pennsylvania.

MALACHITE
Bisbee, Arizona.

MICROCLINE
Variety Amazonstone,
near Florissant, Colorado.

MIMETITE
Variety Campylite,
Dry Gill, Cumberland, England.

ORPIMENT
Mercur, Utah.

PYRITE
Bingham Canyon, Utah.

QUARTZ
Variety Jasper,
Oregon.

QUARTZ
Variety Rock Crystal,
Little Falls, New York.

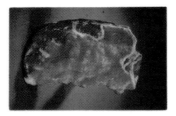

RHODOCHROSITE
Bockenrod, Odenwald,
Germany.

RHODONITE
Variety Fowlerite,
Franklin, New Jersey.

SILVER
Houghton County,
Michigan.

SMITHSONITE
Kelly, New Mexico.

STIBNITE
Ichinokawa, Iyo,
Shikoku Japan.

SULFUR
Cianciana, Sicily.

TOPAZ
Devils Head, Colorado.

TOURMALINE
Madagascar.

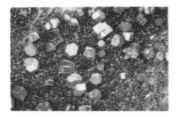

VANADINITE
Near Globe, Arizona.

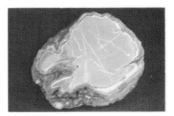

VARISCITE
Fairfield, Utah.

WAVELLITE
Near Hot Springs,
Arkansas.

WOLFRAMITE
Zinnwald, Bohemia.

WULFENITE
Sierra de los Lamentos,
Chihuahua, Mexico.

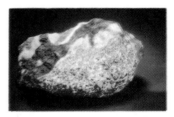

ZINCITE
Franklin, New Jersey.

GYPSUM

KEYS: Nonmetallic luster. Leaves white mark or scratch on streak plate. Shows good cleavage. Can be scratched by fingernail.

Color: White, gray. Specific Gravity: 2.2–2.4 (medium weight).

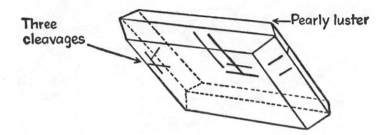

Three cleavages

←Pearly luster

Calcium sulfate ($CaSO_4.2H_2O$) in composition, gypsum is the most common mineral of the sulfate class. Thick beds are known over large areas of the globe, supplying the basic raw material for making plaster of paris. This product gets its name from the gypsum deposits in the Paris basin in France. The crystals from Naica, Mexico, are of colossal size, and those from Wayne County, Utah, and Ellsworth, Ohio, are likewise exceptionally large. Among other clear and nicely formed crystals of gypsum are those from the salt mines at Bex, Switzerland, and Girgenti, Sicily. Transparent gypsum like this is called selenite. Compact material solid enough to be carved into ornaments and useful articles is familiar as alabaster, of which northern Italy and Colorado are the leading sources. Gypsum in veins composed of silky fibers is called satin spar, which has been cut into beads and sold for many years at Niagara Falls. The White Sands in New Mexico, near the rocket proving ground, consist of wind-blown dunes of gypsum sand. Earthy gypsum is called gypsite.

TALC

KEYS: Nonmetallic luster. Leaves white mark or scratch on streak plate. Shows good cleavage. Can be scratched by fingernail.

Color: Green, white.
Specific Gravity: 2.7–2.8 (medium weight).

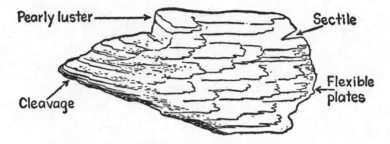

This hydrous magnesium silicate [$Mg_3 (OH)_2 Si_4O_{10}$] is closely related to serpentine. Although the origin of the word talc is lost in obscurity, everyone knows the most familiar product made from this mineral—talcum powder. Owing to its being the softest of all minerals, talc feels soapy. A somewhat more solid form, called soapstone or steatite, is used for chemical sinks and electrical switchboards. Small pieces, called French chalk, are used by tailors to mark cloth. Most of the low-priced objects of Chinese manufacture that are supposed to look like jade are really soapstone, and many of the rest are pyrophyllite, a related mineral grouped with talc when statistics of production are given. Beautiful sea-green specimens of talc come from various places in the Alps; talc from the French Pyrenees is the finest for the cosmetic industry. New York, California, and North Carolina are the leading American sources for talc, which is mined, at intervals, the length of the Appalachian Mountains. Talc combined with other minerals that have grown in it makes interesting specimens.

CALCITE

KEYS: Nonmetallic luster. Leaves white mark or scratch on streak plate. Shows good cleavage. Cannot be scratched by fingernail, but can be scratched by copper coin.

Color: White, colorless.
Specific Gravity: 2.7 (medium weight).

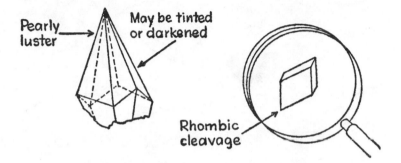

Pearly luster

May be tinted or darkened

Rhombic cleavage

Calcite is calcium carbonate ($CaCO_3$), often very pure. Like all carbonates it fizzes in acid. Describing typical calcite would be difficult, for over 300 forms and more than 1,000 combinations have been recorded. Hence calcite may have almost any outward appearance, but it always breaks into fragments of one shape, the rhomb. Fortunately, some kinds of calcite crystals turn up frequently enough to become familiar. Absolutely clear pieces of calcite, first found in Iceland, are called Iceland spar; they have the interesting property of making a line seem double when viewed through them. One crystal of this variety from near Helgustadir, Iceland, measured 20 feet in length. Several crystals weighing more than 25 tons each have come from near Taos, in New Mexico. The golden calcite from Joplin, Mo., is little short of spectacular, as are the resplendent crystals from several localities in northern England. "Dogtooth spar" and "nailhead spar" owe their names to peculiar forms of calcite crystals.

DOLOMITE

KEYS: Nonmetallic luster. Leaves white mark or scratch on streak plate. Shows good cleavage. Cannot be scratched by fingernail, but can be scratched by copper coin.

Color: Pink, white.

Specific Gravity: 2.8–2.9 (medium weight).

The calcium–magnesium carbonate [CaMg(CO₃)₂] is called dolomite after Déodat de Dolomieu (1750–1801), a French engineer and mineralogist. Being a carbonate, it fizzes in acid, though less vigorously than calcite and though the acid may have to be warmed. Beds of dolomite of considerable thickness have been deposited in many parts of the world, where they may be used as building stone. Ordinary limestone turns to dolomite upon the addition of magnesium from any one of a number of underground sources. Large transparent dolomite crystals of choice quality occur near Djelfa, Algeria. Dolomite grows on the inside of the intriguing hollow rocks which are so abundant near Keokuk, Iowa; called geodes, they resemble rough, rocky balls until they are broken open, when they reveal a glitter of many tiny crystals. Large crystals of dolomite come from Roxbury, Vt. The mineral is found in cavities in rock at Niagara Falls, Lockport, and Rochester, N.Y. A good deal of translucent dolomite surrounds the lead and zinc minerals at Joplin, Mo.

BARITE

KEYS: Nonmetallic luster. Leaves white mark or scratch on streak plate. Shows good cleavage. Cannot be scratched by fingernail, but can be scratched by copper coin.

Color: White, colorless, blue.

Specific Gravity: 4.5 (heavy).

Diamond-shaped cleavage

Vitreous luster

Barite is barium sulfate ($BaSO_4$), the most common mineral containing barium and one of the most common sulfate minerals. Its name appropriately means "heavy." Crystals of an enchanting blue color can be collected in abundance at two localities in Colorado, near Hartsel and Sterling. Reddish-brown flowerlike groups, such as those from Norman, Okla., are called barite roses. A single transparent crystal weighing 100 pounds was taken from a lead mine in Westmorland County, England. Large quantities of white barite, carrying brown stains in cracks and corners, are typical of the commercial deposits in Missouri. Stalactites of brown barite are found at Newhaven, England. In the Bad Lands of South Dakota crystals of barite have grown in distorted shapes inside the hollow bones of fossil animals buried there for millions of years. Barite localities are numerous in California. For its home this mineral favors limestone and metal-bearing veins. The most important use of barite is in the drilling of wells.

CELESTITE

KEYS: Nonmetallic luster. Leaves white mark or scratch on streak plate. Shows good cleavage. Cannot be scratched by fingernail, but can be scratched by copper coin.

Color: Blue, colorless, white.
Specific Gravity: 3.9–4.0 (heavy).

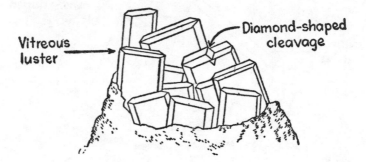

Vitreous luster

Diamond-shaped cleavage

Celestite is strontium sulfate ($SrSO_4$) and was given its name because the first specimens, found near Bellwood, Pa., were a celestial blue. This color, though frequent enough in most places, is not an essential characteristic, however. In a cave at historic Put in Bay in Lake Erie excellent crystals over 18 inches long have been discovered. Daintily fashioned groups of crystals are collected at Clay Center, Ohio. The celestite in the sulfur beds at Girgenti, Sicily, is doubtless the best known. Complex blue crystals occur in cavities in copper mines at Herrengrund, Czechoslovakia. Large crystals are found at Lampasas, Tex. Some fossils are seen to have changed to celestite as a result of petrifaction under special geologic conditions. This mineral and barite often look exactly alike, especially when they have a tinge of blue. Then perhaps the best way to tell them apart is to hold a piece in a very hot flame, which will become green for barite or red for celestite when the mineral begins to decompose.

HALITE

KEYS: Nonmetallic luster. Leaves white mark or scratch on streak plate. Shows good cleavage. Cannot be scratched by fingernail, but can be scratched by copper coin.

Color: Colorless, white. Specific Gravity: 2.2 (light).

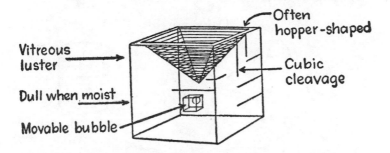

Vitreous luster

Dull when moist

Movable bubble

Often hopper-shaped

Cubic cleavage

As a mineral, sodium chloride (NaCl) is called halite, but it is still the familiar table salt. Vast beds of such rock salt, and huge bodies called salt domes abound. Well-crystallized specimens have come from Stassfurt, Germany, and Bochnia, Poland, as well as several places on the island of Sicily. Peculiar distorted crystals are found in Humboldt County, Nev. Attractive masses of superior transparency are obtained in the Verde Valley, Ariz. A curious feature of many halite crystals is the hopper-shaped opening that penetrates the faces. Interesting, also, are the occasional hollow spots inside, containing a drop of water which moves back and forth like the bubble in a carpenter's spirit level. The salty taste of halite is a distinctive property of it, and of course it dissolves easily in water. Some halite is blue, possibly owing to the displacement of atoms in the structure. Contrary to general belief, most halite is used in the chemical industry rather than as food, but its use to sustain life cannot be dispensed with.

103

CRYOLITE

KEYS: Nonmetallic luster. Leaves white mark or scratch on streak plate. Shows good cleavage. Cannot be scratched by fingernail, but can be scratched by copper coin.

Color: Colorless, white.

Specific Gravity: 3.0 (medium weight).

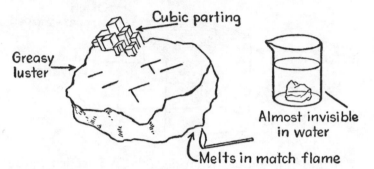

Cubic parting

Greasy luster

Almost invisible in water

Melts in match flame

Natural sodium–aluminum fluoride (Na_3AlF_6) is cryolite. The early Norsemen who visited Greenland were astonished to find the Eskimos using as anchors a heavy stone which disappeared when lowered into the sea. Cryolite has the strange property of being almost invisible in water, because it has nearly the same light-bending power as water, and rays of light pass through it in a straight line. Its name means "frost stone," in allusion to its icy appearance. It can be melted in a candle flame. The occurrence of cryolite in Greenland is the more remarkable because the mineral is extremely rare except there; but at Ivigtut in Arksuk Fjord on the west coast it is found in an enormous deposit. Associated with the cryolite are a number of rare fluorine-bearing minerals derived from it, and some common ore minerals. The cryolite is taken to Denmark for processing, and it is used as an insecticide and in the aluminum industry. Very limited amounts have also been found near Miask, Siberia; Sallent, Spain; and Colorado Springs, Colo.

ANHYDRITE

KEYS: Nonmetallic luster. Leaves white mark or scratch on streak plate. Shows good cleavage. Cannot be scratched by fingernail, but can be scratched by copper coin.

Color: White. Specific Gravity: 2.9–3.0 (medium weight).

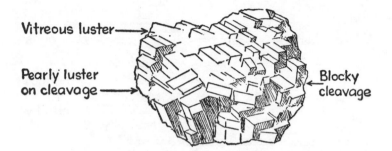

Vitreous luster ⟶

Pearly luster on cleavage ⟶

Blocky cleavage

Its composition being calcium sulfate ($CaSO_4$), anhydrite in 1803 received its name because it does not contain water, as does gypsum, which otherwise has the same chemical formula. At Lockport, N.Y., fine blue anhydrite is found in cavities in limestone, and good crystals occur at Stassfurt, Germany. At times anhydrite appears in veins with metallic minerals and in the gas cavities of volcanic rocks. It occurs mostly, however, in large masses, together with rock salt and gypsum, which are likewise deposited by the evaporation of sea water in isolated arms of the ocean. Either anhydrite or gypsum will precipitate from the same solution, according to the temperature of the water, the salt content, and other factors; afterward anhydrite may change into gypsum by adding water, or gypsum may change into anhydrite by losing it. Thick beds of anhydrite are situated near Carlsbad National Park, N.M., and in the adjacent part of Texas. Nova Scotia also contains extensive beds. On Calumet Island, Que., anhydrite has replaced marble of very great geologic age.

105

KERNITE

KEYS: Nonmetallic luster. Leaves white mark or scratch on streak plate. Shows good cleavage. Cannot be scratched by fingernail, but can be scratched by copper coin.
Color: Colorless, white. Specific Gravity: 1.9 (light).

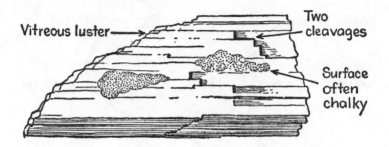

Vitreous luster⟶

Two cleavages

Surface often chalky

Kernite, a hydrous sodium borate $(Na_2B_4O_7.4H_2O)$, is now the chief commercial source of borax. Found in 1926 and named after Kern County, Calif., kernite was not known anywhere else in the world. It occurs near Kramer in the Mojave Desert, in a deposit containing millions of tons. This is the unusual circumstance of a new mineral's being discovered in huge quantities at the start. Kernite is associated with the mineral borax, from which it is believed to have altered by contact with heated rocks that forced themselves up into a buried lake from beneath. The largest single crystal measured 8 feet long and 3 feet wide, and many others are several feet thick. When in contact with other borate minerals, the surface of kernite turns chalky white, but isolated specimens do not behave this way. This coating is tincalconite, named from the ancient Oriental word for borax powder. When placed in water, kernite becomes white and opaque, and then dissolves—slowly in cold water, more rapidly in hot water.

ANGLESITE

KEYS: Nonmetallic luster. Leaves white mark or scratch on streak plate. Shows good cleavage. Cannot be scratched by fingernail, but can be scratched by copper coin.

Color: Colorless, white, gray.

Specific Gravity: 6.2–6.4 (very heavy).

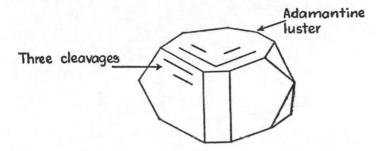

Adamantine luster

Three cleavages

Anglesite, which is lead sulfate ($PbSO_4$), results from the oxidation of galena and is often recognized as a gray band enclosing a core of still-shiny galena, which has been preserved from change. Another lead mineral which forms at the same time is cerussite, which may in turn alter from the anglesite. Interesting to find are cavities in galena lined with crystals of anglesite and sulfur. Though much less important than galena, anglesite is also used as an ore of lead. Large amounts are mined in Mexico and Australia. Crystals are embedded in sulfur at Los Lamentos, Mexico. Superlative crystals have come from Sidi-Amor-ben-Salem, Tunis. The crystals from Monte Poni, Sardinia, are also of exciting quality. The original locality after which the mineral was named is the island of Anglesey in the Irish Sea; but the specimens there were small, although good ones have been obtained from Pary's mine. In the United States the largest are those labeled Wheatley mine, Phoenixville, Pa.

SODALITE

KEYS: Nonmetallic luster. Leaves white mark or scratch on streak plate. Shows good cleavage. Cannot be scratched by copper coin, but can be scratched by knife blade.

Color: Blue. **Specific Gravity:** 2.2–2.4 (medium weight).

Vitreous luster

Six cleavages

Sodalite is a sodium-aluminum silicate [$Na_4(AlSiO_4)_3Cl$]. A test for the chlorine it contains is often needed for an accurate identification of this mineral, particularly if it happens not to be blue. The name, adopted in 1811, refers to the sodium that is present. The rich blue color of sodalite makes it a satisfying ornamental stone. Masses of this select quality occur in Canada on Ice River near Kicking Horse Pass, B.C.; Dungannon, Ont.; and several places in Quebec. Litchfield, Me., and Salem, Mass., are American sources. Unusual transparent white crystals are found in the lavas of Mount Vesuvius. Sodalite is a member of the feldspathoid group of minerals, so called because they take the place of feldspar in certain rocks that are deficient in silica. Other feldspathoid minerals that also have a deep-blue color, but are less abundant, are lazurite, noselite, and hauynite—this last one constituting most of the gemmy rock known as lapis lazuli, which is marked by white streaks of calcite and golden flecks of pyrite and was known to antiquity as sapphire.

PYROXENE

KEYS: Nonmetallic luster. Leaves white mark or scratch on streak plate. Shows good cleavage. Cannot be scratched by copper coin, but can be scratched by knife blade.

Color: Black, green, white.

Specific Gravity: 3.2–3.4 (medium weight).

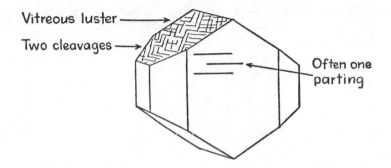

Vitreous luster

Two cleavages

Often one parting

Pyroxene is one of the most important groups of minerals, the essential constituent of many rocks formed at high temperatures. The members of the group are all silicates but vary in composition considerably among themselves. Jadeite, the preferred of the two kinds of true jade, is a pyroxene found mainly in Upper Burma. Spodumene is remarkable because of its enormous crystals, some individuals from near Keystone, S.D., measuring 40 feet or more in length and weighing up to 90 tons. A delicate variety of spodumene, cut into lovely pinkish-violet gems, is kunzite, found mostly at Pala, Calif., and in Madagascar. Diopside, another pyroxene, occurs largely in marble, as do the clear crystals at Ala, Italy. Enstatite is common in meteorites, and grades into hypersthene as the percentage of iron increases. Of all the pyroxenes, however, the one by far the likeliest to turn up is augite; hence this is the one illustrated above. Crystals of it are common in the volcanic cinders of the Hawaiian Islands and elsewhere.

AMPHIBOLE

KEYS: Nonmetallic luster. Leaves white mark or scratch on streak plate. Shows good cleavage. Cannot be scratched by copper coin, but can be scratched by knife blade.

Color: Black, green, white.

Specific Gravity: 2.9–3.4 (medium weight).

Vitreous luster——→ 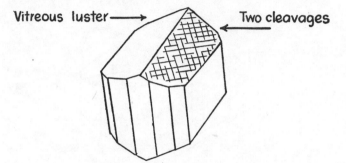 ←—— Two cleavages

Amphibole is a group of minerals related to pyroxene and of great importance as constituents of rocks. Unlike the pyroxenes they yield some water when sufficiently heated, and their crystals tend toward being six-sided rather than squarish. In composition they are complex silicates, hornblende, the most common of them, having a chemical formula nearly as long as a line of type in this book. Hornblende is taken as the typical amphibole and is illustrated here, but the other minerals of the group have the same oblique cleavage and are thereby distinguished from pyroxene. Arfvedsonite is a sodium-rich amphibole found in large crystals near Julianehaab, Greenland. Glaucophane, occurring in the Coast Ranges of California, has also a high content of sodium but a distinctive blue color. Anthophyllite, named from the Latin word for clove because of its clove-brown color, is one of the simpler amphiboles. White tremolite grades into green actinolite; when either of them is compact and tough, it is called nephrite, which is a true jade.

KYANITE

KEYS: Nonmetallic luster. Leaves white mark or scratch on streak plate. Shows good cleavage. Cannot be scratched by copper coin, but can be scratched by knife blade.

Color: Blue, white.

Specific Gravity: 3.5–3.7 (medium weight).

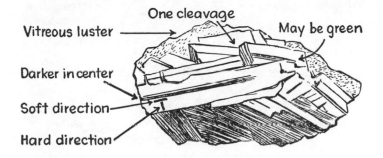

An aluminum silicate (Al_2SiO_5), kyanite has a chemical composition identical with those of andalusite and sillimanite. When heated to the neighborhood of 1000°C., it becomes a substance called mullite, which furnishes a heat-defying and shock-resisting porcelain used for spark plugs and chemical ware. The variable hardness of kyanite, whereby it can be scratched by a knife along the "grain" but resists being scratched in the perpendicular direction, is a unique characteristic. Its attractive bicolored, blade-shaped crystals are the principal reason, however, for its strong appeal to the mineral collector. The name kyanite refers to its blue color, which is often in spots or streaks. Beautiful combinations of kyanite and staurolite occur at Monte Campione, Switzerland. The clear green crystals from Yancey County, N. C., are different but none the less lovely. The chief commercial deposits are at Lapsa Bura, India, and in Kenya, the British colony in East Africa.

FLUORITE

KEYS: Nonmetallic luster. Leaves white mark or scratch on streak plate. Shows good cleavage. Cannot be scratched by copper coin, but can be scratched by knife blade.

Color: Purple, light-green, yellow.

Specific Gravity: 3.2 (medium weight).

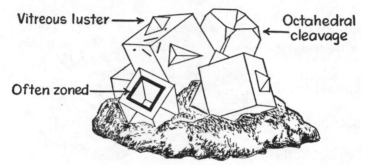

Vitreous luster ⟶

⟵ Octahedral cleavage

Often zoned

Calcium fluoride (CaF_2) is called fluorite. Although it is the mineral that gave its name to fluorescence, this interesting effect is weakly shown. Superb crystal groups come from noted English localities, including Castleton in Derbyshire and Cleator Moor in Cumberland. From Derbyshire, also, came the prized blue john, a banded blue variety which was carved into vases. Large sea-green cubes are found at Muscalonge Lake, N.Y. Pretty brown crystals come from Clay Center, Ohio. The gorgeous purple specimens from near Rosiclare, Ill., are indeed outstanding; some of the large, clear crystals look almost like stained-glass church windows when the sun gleams through. Clear, colorless crystals come from Modoc, Ont. Scarcely any lovely hue—plum, rose, any you prefer—is missing from the colors that fluorite may possess. This mineral received its name from the Latin word meaning "to flow" because it melts at a low temperature; today its main use is as a flux to help melt iron ore when making steel.

RHODONITE

KEYS: Nonmetallic luster. Leaves white mark or scratch on streak plate. Shows good cleavage. Cannot be scratched by copper coin, but can be scratched by knife blade.

Color: Rose-red, pink, brown.

Specific Gravity: 3.4–3.7 (medium weight).

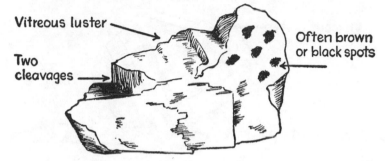

Given its name from the Greek word for a rose, on account of its rose-pink color, rhodonite is manganese silicate ($MnSiO_3$). Large quantities of it have been mined near Sverdlovsk (formerly Ekaterinburg) in the Ural Mountains and were extensively used in old Russia as an ornamental stone. Among the best-known sources of rhodonite crystals are Franklin, N.J.; Långban, Sweden; and Broken Hill, New South Wales. The New Jersey variety contains zinc and is also called fowlerite. The black coating on the surface of typical specimens is the result of an external alteration to manganese oxide, which may extend along cracks within the mineral. Rhodonite is a minor ore of manganese, generally when it is associated with other minerals of greater economic importance. Rhodonite looks like pink feldspar, which is lighter in weight; and somewhat like rhodochrosite, which is a carbonate and has a different cleavage. It also resembles the pyroxene minerals in crystallization but is no longer regarded as belonging to the same group.

RHODOCHROSITE

KEYS: Nonmetallic luster. Leaves white mark or scratch on streak plate. Shows good cleavage. Cannot be scratched by copper coin, but can be scratched by knife blade.

Color: Rose-red, pink.

Specific Gravity: 3.3–3.6 (medium weight).

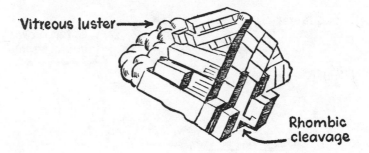

Vitreous luster

Rhombic cleavage

Manganese carbonate (MgCO₃) is rhodochrosite, so named because of its lovely rose-red color. Like other carbonate minerals it fizzes when a drop of acid is applied, and finally dissolves completely in warm acid. Rhodochrosite is an important ore of manganese at Butte, Mont., but has only a little use elsewhere. Unrivaled crystals, almost ruby-red in color and clarity, have come from old silver mines in central Colorado. Rhodochrosite is a common mineral in the silver mines at Austin, Nev. It is also found elsewhere in the United States, especially at Branchville, Conn., and Franklin, N.J. In Europe the leading localities include Kapnik, Rumania, and Freiberg, Germany, where it occurs in silver veins. Rhodochrosite is softer than rhodonite, which likewise has a pink color. A black or brown surface covering indicates chemical alteration. Apart from its color, it has the appearance of calcite, dolomite, siderite, and smithsonite, which are all carbonate minerals belonging to the same group and having the same rhombohedral cleavage.

SIDERITE

KEYS: Nonmetallic luster. Leaves white mark or scratch on streak plate. Shows good cleavage. Cannot be scratched by copper coin, but can be scratched by knife blade.

Color: Brown. Specific Gravity: 3.8–3.9 (heavy).

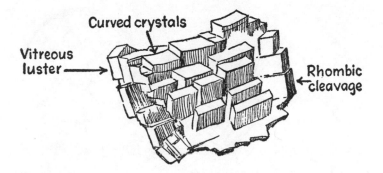

Curved crystals

Vitreous luster →

← Rhombic cleavage

Iron carbonate (FeCO₃) is known as siderite from the Greek word meaning iron. Spathic iron and chalybite are miners' names for this mineral. The tendency of siderite crystals to seem curved is worth noting, for this property is restricted to only a few minerals, including dolomite. The specimens from many of the mines in Cornwall, England, are exceptionally good; the six-sided plates from Wheal Maudlin are evenly developed and highly attractive. Good crystals also occur at Brosso, Italy, and Allevard, France. A deposit of economic value is situated at Styria, Austria, and siderite is also mined in Great Britain, but the proportion of iron is too low for it to be used very much in most countries, where better ores are available. Veins of lead and silver ores in Idaho contain much siderite. Impure siderite, mixed with clay and known as clay ironstone, is distributed through the coal beds that extend from Pennsylvania to Ohio. Siderite alters readily to other minerals, especially goethite, which retain the original siderite shape.

115

STRONTIANITE

KEYS: Nonmetallic luster. Leaves white mark or scratch on streak plate. Shows good cleavage. Cannot be scratched by copper coin, but can be scratched by knife blade.

Color: White. Specific Gravity: 3.7 (medium weight).

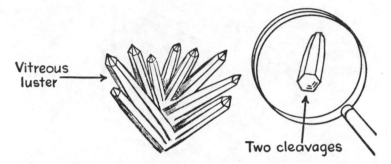

Vitreous luster

Two cleavages

As carbonate of strontium ($SrCO_3$), strontianite gave its name in 1790 to the chemical element of which it is one source of supply. Like other carbonate minerals it fizzes in acid. The original locality was Strontian, Scotland, the town after which it received its name. The biggest deposits are situated in Germany at Drensteinfurt, Ascheberg, and Ahlen, and these have yielded fine crystals. Well-proportioned crystals occur in the lead mines at Pateley Bridge, England; strontianite is sometimes associated in this way with metals in veins, more especially in Germany and also in Mexico. Nests and spheres of crystals are found at Schoharie, N.Y. Good-sized deposits occur in the Strontium Hills, north of Barstow, Calif., and the mineral comes from other places in that state. In Texas strontianite occurs on Mount Bonnell (near Austin) and in the cap rock that overlies the salt domes along the Gulf of Mexico. In Washington it is collected near La Conner. Strontianite resembles aragonite in its over-all nature, except that it is much less likely to form in distinct crystals.

SMITHSONITE

KEYS: Nonmetallic luster. Leaves white mark or scratch
on streak plate. Shows good cleavage. Cannot be
scratched by copper coin, but can be scratched by
knife blade.

Color: White, brown, green. Specific Gravity: 4.4 (heavy).

Vitreous luster →

Often fibrous →

Rhombic cleavage

Smithsonite, zinc carbonate ($ZnCO_3$), is one of the most variable of all minerals in appearance. Some of its varieties are so disguised that they do not look a bit like smithsonite. Take, for example, the so-called dry-bone ore, which, of course, resembles a dried bone; it is mined in the zinc district of Wisconsin-Illinois-Iowa. Another curious variety is turkey-fat ore, yellow in color because it contains cadmium; stalactites of it, with concentric banding, come from Sardinia. White spheres of smithsonite are found in the mines in the province of Santander, Spain. Probably the most appealing smithsonite is a rich green, solid enough for gem cutting, and coming from Kelly, N.M. Several of the smithsonite colors are associated together at Laurium, Greece. Matchless crystals have come from Rhodesia. Large deposits of smithsonite occur in Germany. This mineral was named in 1832 in honor of the Englishman James Smithson (1765–1829), who founded the Smithsonian Institution in Washington; in England it used to be called calamine.

117

STILBITE

KEYS: Nonmetallic luster. Leaves white mark or scratch on streak plate. Shows good cleavage. Cannot be scratched by copper coin, but can be scratched by knife blade.

Color: White. Specific Gravity: 2.1–2.2 (light).

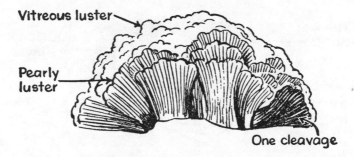

An aluminum silicate with a complex formula, stilbite is one of the numerous attractive members of the zeolite family, all of which are characterized by the fact that they give off water in copious amounts at a steady rate when they are heated. Its distinctive form is that of sheaflike groups of crystals, which spread out at both ends. Single, untwinned crystals are not known, but twins of stilbite often resemble a tabular crystal—a common type of occurrence. The name stilbite comes from the Greek word for luster, in reference to the pearly luster on the faces that correspond to the cleavage surfaces. Stilbite occurs with other zeolites in cavities in lava rocks which have cooled upon or near the surface of the earth. Fine-quality specimens of stilbite are numerous in northern New Jersey, in Nova Scotia, and at Guanajuato, Mexico. Large salmon-colored tabular crystals are found at Poona, India. Peerless white crystals of the same shape line cavities in the basalt of the Faeroe Islands, in the North Atlantic Ocean. The desirable crystals from Kilpatrick, Scotland, are red.

118

HEMIMORPHITE

KEYS: Nonmetallic luster. Leaves white mark or scratch on streak plate. Shows good cleavage. Cannot be scratched by copper coin, but can be scratched by knife blade.

Color: Colorless, white.

Specific Gravity: 3.4–3.5 (medium weight).

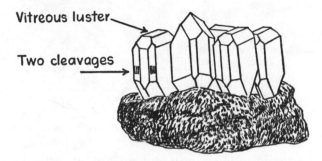

Vitreous luster

Two cleavages

Hemimorphite, a hydrous silicate of zinc [$Zn_4Si_2O_7(OH)_2 \cdot H_2O$], has been the innocent victim of a confusion in names which has also involved other zinc minerals. Most mining people still call it calamine, but the scientific name of hemimorphite was suggested to apply solely to this one mineral. It refers to the fact that the crystals are developed in halves, the opposite ends being different from each other. This sometimes produces a peculiar effect of unbalance and lack of symmetry as the sheaflike groups are examined closely, and the pointed ends of the individual crystals are seen to be attached to the rock. The glossy crystals from the old zinc mines at Aachen, Germany, are well known. Truly splendid crystals have come from Djebel Guergour, Algeria. Elkhorn, Mont., and Granby, Mo., are American localities for fine specimens. Hemimorphite serves as a significant ore of zinc. It is a secondary mineral, originating from the action of silica-bearing water upon other zinc minerals. Its closest companion is smithsonite.

NATROLITE

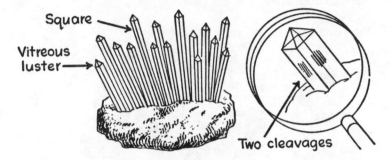

This hydrous silicate of sodium and aluminum, with the formula $Na_2Al_2Si_3O_{10}·2H_2O$, is one of the zeolite minerals, with their property of becoming dehydrated at a constant rate upon being heated. Its name alludes to its sodium content. As one of the last minerals to solidify, natrolite incrusts the surface of cracks and cavities in volcanic rocks, along with other zeolites and calcite. The radiating groups of slender crystals are so typical that natrolite has been called needle zeolite. It fuses more easily than aragonite, for which it might be taken. Among the largest of all known specimens are the dazzling white crystals that used to come from Puy de Marman, France. Large crystals come from British Columbia's Ice Valley, and needles several inches long are known at Bishopton, Scotland. Fine specimens occur in the trap quarries at Weehawken and other towns in New Jersey, and in the renowned zeolite-bearing rocks of Nova Scotia. Aussig, Czechoslovakia, is another important locality for natrolite.

COLEMANITE

KEYS: Nonmetallic luster. Leaves white mark or scratch on streak plate. Shows good cleavage. Cannot be scratched by copper coin, but can be scratched by knife blade.

Color: Colorless, white.

Specific Gravity: 2.4 (medium weight).

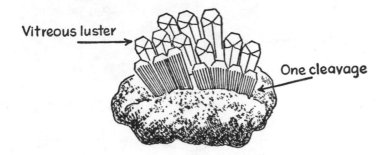

Vitreous luster

One cleavage

The handsomest of the borate minerals is colemanite, a hydrous calcium borate $(Ca_2B_6O_{11}.5H_2O)$. The brilliant clear crystals, up to several inches in length, often occur as a lining inside porcelainlike chunks of the same mineral. The crystals look rather like calcite but have a brighter luster. Rounded masses, however, are the usual mode of occurrence. First noticed in Death Valley in 1883 and furnishing the main supply of the world's borax at the time of the discovery of kernite in 1926, colemanite is found as a buried lake deposit in a number of counties in southern California and western Nevada. It is believed to be an alteration of ulexite, a mineral sometimes known as cotton-ball borax because it forms in soft, rounded, white masses of loose texture. A little colemanite is found in Siberia and Argentina. A most interesting occurrence is in a fossil egg picked up along the Gila River in Arizona. Colemanite bears the name of a founder of the California borax industry, William T. Coleman, of San Francisco.

APOPHYLLITE

KEYS: Nonmetallic luster. Leaves white mark or scratch on streak plate. Shows good cleavage. Cannot be scratched by copper coin, but can be scratched by knife blade.

Color: Colorless, white.

Specific Gravity: 2.3–2.4 (medium weight).

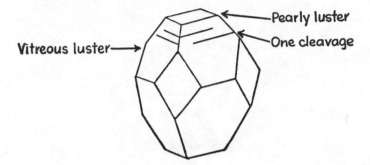

Vitreous luster⟶

Pearly luster

One cleavage

A silicate mineral containing a large amount of water [$Ca_4K(Si_4O_{10})_2F.8H_2O$], apophyllite was named from the fact that it unfolds like a leaf when it is heated. Its whitish-pearly look has been described as like the eye of a boiled fish, and it once bore a much weirder name which meant "fish eye." The natural home of apophyllite is in cavities in basalt and other lava rocks, in many localities throughout the world. It is thus associated with the zeolite minerals, which it resembles in many ways. The largest and most beautiful crystals of this mineral were uncovered during the construction of a railroad at Poona, India. Good-sized crystals stained with bitumin occur in the New Almaden mercury mines in California. Delicate pink specimens are found in the silver veins at Andreasberg in the Harz Mountains, Germany, and appealing crystals of the same tint rest firmly upon amethyst at Guanajuato, Mexico. The volcanic rocks near Paterson, N.J., near Philadelphia, Pa., and in northern Michigan yield apophyllite.

WOLLASTONITE

KEYS: Nonmetallic luster. Leaves white mark or scratch on streak plate. Shows good cleavage. Cannot be scratched by copper coin, but can be scratched by knife blade.

Color: White. Specific Gravity: 2.8–2.9 (medium weight).

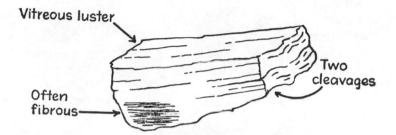

Vitreous luster

Two cleavages

Often fibrous

Wollastonite is calcium silicate ($CaSiO_3$). Named in 1818 in recognition of the work of the English chemist William Hyde Wollaston (1766-1828), its name is easy to remember when you know that it is pronounced to rhyme with "wool" and that this mineral is used industrially as raw material in the making of rock wool for insulation. Wollastonite is one of the interesting minerals referred to as geologic thermometers because they indicate the temperature at which they must have originated within the rocky crust of the earth. Wherever wollastonite is found, the temperature there is known to have been below about 1125°C., because above that point a different kind of calcium silicate is formed instead. Large white crystals of wollastonite are common at Diana, N.Y. Showy crystals line some of the cavities in blocks thrown out by the volcanic explosions of Mount Vesuvius. Crestmore, Calif., is a noted locality for large amounts of wollastonite, as well as for a diversity of unusual minerals scarcely equaled anywhere else. A compact variety of wollastonite is found in Isle Royale National Park, Mich.

EPIDOTE

Keys: Nonmetallic luster. Leaves white mark or scratch on streak plate. Shows good cleavage. Can scratch glass and be scratched by quartz.
Color: Yellowish-green, blackish-green.
Specific Gravity: 3.3–3.5 (medium weight).

Vitreous luster

Crystals darker than rock

One cleavage

Parallel grooves

Epidote, a hydrous silicate mineral [$Ca_2 (Al,Fe)_3 (SiO_4)_3$-OH], occurs in many localities. When found in good crystals, it is a most attractive mineral, in spite of its typical, rather monotonous yellowish-green color, which is often described as pistachio-green and is a fairly distinctive property for identifying epidote. This color grades into brownish-green, gray, and black, though it may be red or even disappear entirely in the very rare colorless specimens from remote Tierra del Fuego at the tip of South America. Magnificent dark-green crystals, transparent and lustrous, are present in rock cavities near Salzburg, Austria. On Prince of Wales Island, Alaska, are found dark crystals of extraordinary size and beauty, which have dominated the market in recent years. Other excellent crystals carry labels reading Haddam, Conn., and Bourg d'Oisans, France. Those from the Zillerthal, Austria, are sometimes rose-red in color. Epidote is associated with native copper in northern Michigan, as a product of alteration from other minerals. Clear epidote, when cut into gems, is dark-green in one direction and brown in another.

124

FELDSPAR

KEYS: Nonmetallic luster. Leaves white mark or scratch on streak plate. Shows good cleavage. Can scratch glass and be scratched by quartz.

Color: White, pink.

Specific Gravity: 2.6–2.8 (medium weight).

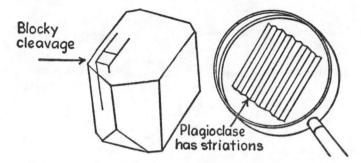

Blocky cleavage

Plagioclase has striations

Feldspar is a group of minerals of the greatest scientific importance. All members of the group are aluminum silicates and have varying amounts of other chemical elements, especially potassium, sodium, and calcium. The feldspars resemble one another so closely that they usually have to be identified with a microscope. It is customary to divide them into two main types—plagioclase and potash feldspar. Plagioclase is recognized by the presence of a series of closely spaced straight lines on the cleavage surface. This type has been arbitrarily divided into six members, of which albite and labradorite are the best known, but only labradorite can be named at sight, owing to its dark color and radiant blue sheen which spreads across the surface as the specimen is turned. Of the other type, called potash feldspar, the chief members are orthoclase and microcline. If the specimen is a clear crystal, it is orthoclase; if green, it is sure to be microcline—the attractive variety called amazonstone, most abundant in the Pikes Peak region of Colorado. The feldspars are the most common of all minerals.

CORUNDUM

KEYS: Nonmetallic luster. Leaves white mark or scratch on streak plate. Shows good cleavage. Cannot be scratched by quartz.

Color: Bluish-gray, brown, pink, blue.

Specific Gravity: 4.0 (heavy).

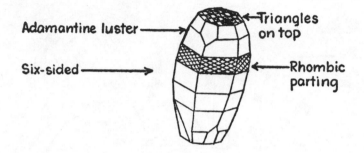

Adamantine luster → Triangles on top

Six-sided → Rhombic parting

Corundum is aluminum oxide (Al_2O_3). Its hardness, surpassing that of all other minerals except diamond, enables it to serve as an abrasive, but its real value lies in the beauty of its colors. Few of us would think that the fiery red of ruby and the serene blue of sapphire belong to the same mineral, unless we were to see the original crystals. Sapphires of yellow, green, purple, and other colors are also corundum. The Orient—Ceylon, Kashmir, Burma, Siam—is the favored home of all these gems, but they are found in Australia and elsewhere as well. A prized variation of corundum is a star ruby or star sapphire. Large rough crystals of ordinary corundum come from Steinkopf, South Africa, and from the districts of Zoutpansberg and Pietersburg, Transvaal—a jumbo-sized specimen from Pietersburg weighed 335 pounds. Corundum is abundant in parts of North Carolina, South Carolina, and Georgia, and in Ontario, Canada. When it is intimately mixed with magnetite, the natural product is called emery, a useful grinding material coming chiefly from Turkey and islands off the coast of Greece.

TOPAZ

KEYS: Nonmetallic luster. Leaves white mark or scratch on streak plate. Shows good cleavage. Cannot be scratched by quartz.

Color: Colorless, yellow, blue.

Specific Gravity: 3.4–3.6 (medium weight).

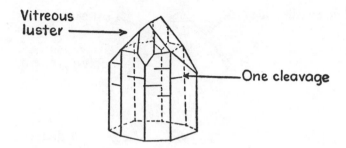

Vitreous luster ⟶

One cleavage

Topaz, an aluminum silicate with fluorine [Al_2SiO_4 (F,-OH)$_2$], constitutes one of the major gem minerals. Although usually thought of as a yellow stone, topaz is more apt to occur in some other color, of which blue and pink are certainly the loveliest. Many crystals fade upon exposure to much sunlight, and others can be altered by heat to produce hues that are more salable. Enormous crystals, colorless and blue, and weighing hundreds of pounds each, have come from the state of Minas Gerais, Brazil, in late years. Charming peach-colored crystals, which soon lose all traces of color in the bright desert sun, can be obtained in almost unlimited numbers in the Thomas Range of western Utah. Large blue crystals come from cavities on the steep slopes of Pikes Peak, Colo. Those from Mason County, Tex., are similarly fine. The deep-wine crystals from south of Nerchinsk, Siberia, make outstanding specimens. The word Topazion, from which topaz is derived, is the name of an island in the Red Sea between Egypt and Arabia, but previously was applied to a different mineral.

DIAMOND

KEYS: Nonmetallic luster. Leaves white mark or scratch on streak plate. Shows good cleavage. Cannot be scratched by quartz.

Color: Colorless, white, gray.

Specific Gravity: 3.4 (medium weight).

Pure carbon in composition (C), diamond is the hardest of all known substances, the most popular of all gems, and scientifically the most remarkable of all minerals. Industrial diamonds are unexcelled for their ability to cut anything from granite rock to other diamonds. The word diamond comes from the Greek language and means invincible, in reference to this extraordinary power. With their sensitive cleavage, however, gem diamonds cannot be subjected to sudden blows, in spite of their resistance to scratching—this fact is the basis for the convenient method used to cleave diamond crystals in order to remove flaws and prepare the stones for faceting. India was long the principal source of diamond and furnished most of the famous stones of history. In the eighteenth century it was replaced by Brazil as the leading producer, a position assumed by South Africa in about 1870. The Congo nation is today the chief supplier of industrial diamond. A considerable yield of diamond has come from Pike County, Ark., in currently unproductive fields.

SULFUR

KEYS: Nonmetallic luster. Leaves white mark or scratch on streak plate. Does not show good cleavage. Can be scratched by fingernail.

Color: Yellow. Fracture: Even.

Specific Gravity: 2.1 (light).

Resinous luster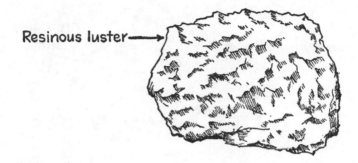

Known to the ancients as brimstone, native sulfur (S) is a mineral of widespread occurrence. To the mineral collector, any of the bright yellow masses are worth having, but the crystals themselves are indeed intriguing. When they are held close to the ear, they can be heard to crackle, on account of the warmth of your hand, because the outer layers expand away from the still-cool interior. Obviously a crystal of sulfur should be handled carefully. The large crystals from Girgenti, Sicily, and nearby are the most beautiful known. Good crystals are found with asphalt at Perticara, Italy. Attractive porous specimens come from Sulphur, Nev. The vast deposits of Louisiana and Texas, which lie above the so-called salt domes and are "mined" by melting the sulfur with superheated steam, furnish much of the world's needs. Rocks in the vicinity of practically every active volcano are coated with sulfur. Orpiment may resemble sulfur, but it has a pronounced cleavage. Sulfur burns easily with a bluish flame, giving off the pungent odor of sulfur dioxide.

BAUXITE

KEYS: Nonmetallic luster. Leaves white mark or scratch on streak plate. Does not show good cleavage. Can be scratched by fingernail.

Color: White, gray, brown. Fracture: Uneven.

Specific Gravity: 2.0–2.6 (medium weight).

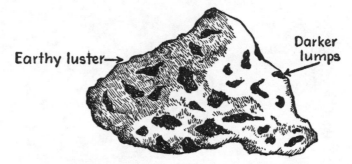

Earthy luster→

Darker lumps

Bauxite has been proved to be a mixture of a number of water-containing aluminum oxide minerals, and not a single mineral as was formerly believed. The constituents are shown by X rays to be mostly gibbsite, boehmite, and diaspore. Still, the name has come into such general use for a highly important commercial substance, and bauxite is usually so uniformly easy to recognize, that we are accustomed to regard it as a mineral instead of a rocklike mixture. The nobby structure is almost always present, the rounded grains varying in size and color; iron is the staining matter. Bauxite originates from the weathering of aluminum-bearing rocks in a warm climate. First discovered at Les Baux, France, it is produced in enormous quantities in Dutch Guiana, British Guiana, and Arkansas and in the Mediterranean countries of Southern Europe. Whether you prefer to think of bauxite as a mineral or a rock, its significance cannot be denied. From it comes most of our supply of the light, strong, conductive, and resistant wonder metal of the twentieth century—aluminum.

KAOLINITE

KEYS: Nonmetallic luster. Leaves white mark or scratch on streak plate. Does not show good cleavage. Can be scratched by fingernail.

Color: White. Fracture: Earthy.

Specific Gravity: 2.6 (medium weight).

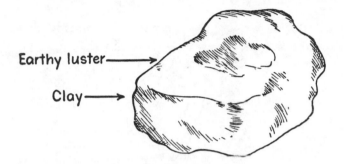

Earthy luster ⟶

Clay ⟶

The best known of the many clay minerals, kaolinite is, like the rest of them, a hydrous aluminum silicate [$Al_2Si_2O_5(OH)_4$]. Other species of clay minerals related to kaolinite include dickite, nacrite, beidellite, montmorillonite, and halloysite. An impure mixture of various of these minerals—often called simply kaolin—is common clay, which is the basis of the porcelain, pottery, and china industries. Both names are a corruption of the Chinese name for a hill near Juachu Fa, where the fine-quality clay was produced from which china was made. Kaolinite is formed by the weathering of rocks that contain a large proportion of feldspar; until the alteration is complete, particles of feldspar are found mixed in the soil as it is being created. The thin crystal plates of kaolinite are seldom large enough to be seen without a microscope; they tend to curl up like dry mud. Masses of kaolinite can often be recognized by a peculiar earthy odor when they are breathed upon, and they become plastic when moistened, adhering slightly to the tongue.

VANADINITE

KEYS: Nonmetallic luster. Leaves white mark or scratch on streak plate. Does not show good cleavage. Cannot be scratched by fingernail, but can be scratched by copper coin.

Color: Orange. Fracture: Uneven.

Specific Gravity: 6.7–7.1 (very heavy).

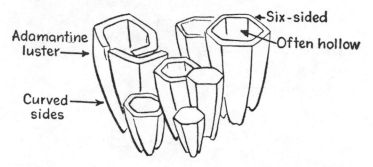

Adamantine luster→

Curved→ sides

←Six-sided

→Often hollow

In composition a vanadate of lead and chlorine (Pb$_5$Cl(VO$_4$)$_3$], vanadinite is an ore of both vanadium and lead. It occurs with other lead minerals, though never in quantity. The most interesting feature of this mineral is its curious crystals. Often they grow in barrel-shaped forms, hollow inside. When straight, they have smooth faces and sharp edges and resemble battlements of a six-sided castle. They look a good deal like crystals of pyromorphite and mimetite, unless their color happens to be quite reddish. Arsenic is a frequent impurity; as it increases, vanadinite becomes the light-yellow variety usually called endlichite. Lustrous yellow and red crystals of vanadinite have been found in Arizona and New Mexico. Those from the Old Yuma mine in Pima County and the Red Cloud mine in Yuma County, both in Arizona, are truly thrilling to see. Zimapán, Mexico, was the first known locality. Large crystals have come from Djebel Mahseur, Morocco, and fine ones also from Grootfontein, South-West Africa.

132

SERPENTINE

KEYS: Nonmetallic luster. Leaves white mark or scratch on streak plate. Does not show good cleavage. Cannot be scratched by fingernail, but can be scratched by copper coin.

Color: Green. **Fracture:** Uneven.

Specific Gravity: 2.5–2.8 (medium weight).

Greasy luster→ 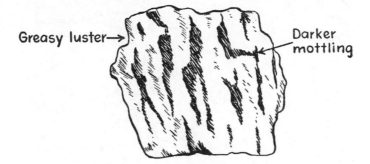 Darker mottling

Serpentine, hydrous magnesium silicate [$Mg_3Si_2O_5(OH)_4$], owes its name to the snakelike pattern of the variegated patches of darker and lighter color that are so typical of it. This mineral may be either platy or fibrous. The platy type is termed antigorite. When fibrous, the variety is called chrysotile, which may have the fibers so well developed as to become true asbestos, although this is not the only asbestos mineral. Thetford, Que., is the asbestos-mining capital of the world. The Canadian deposits extend across the border into New York and Vermont. Among other places, some is even found in the Grand Canyon. Crystals of serpentine are completely unknown, except when they have resulted from the alteration of some older mineral, as, for instance, at the Tilly Foster mine, near Brewster, N.Y. Masses of serpentine have long been used for decorative purposes and as a building stone; a mixture with white carbonate minerals is called verd antique. Serpentine looks like green marble, which, in fact, is often almost solid serpentine.

CERUSSITE

KEYS: Nonmetallic luster. Leaves white mark or scratch on streak plate. Does not show good cleavage. Cannot be scratched by fingernail, but can be scratched by copper coin.

Color: White, gray. **Fracture:** Conchoidal.

Specific Gravity: 6.4–6.6 (very heavy).

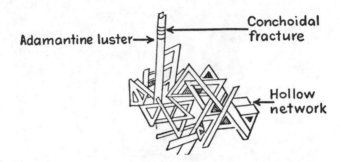

Adamantine luster→

Conchoidal fracture

Hollow network

A lead carbonate ($PbCO_3$), cerussite is an important ore of lead, and sometimes it contains silver which was present in the original mineral, galena, from which it alters. Anglesite, the lead sulfate, sometimes represents an intermediate stage. The Friedrichssegen mine near Ems, Germany, gave us the first known specimens of cerussite. Large crystals of several colors, even including green, have been found at Nerchinsk, Siberia. Groups of crystals shaped like arrowheads come from Broken Hill, New South Wales. Incomparable specimens occur at Tsumeb, South-West Africa. Heart-shaped twins of large size have been collected in Doña Ana County, N.M. Cerussite is abundant at Leadville, Colo., and in the Coeur d'Alene district, Idaho. Its name is derived from the Latin word meaning white lead, an artificial product known by 400 B.C. or earlier; natural cerussite is sometimes called white lead ore. As can be said of all carbonate minerals, cerussite fizzes in acid, but satisfactory results can be had only with nitric acid, which is required to dissolve it.

BORAX

KEYS: Nonmetallic luster. Leaves white mark or scratch on streak plate. Does not show good cleavage. Cannot be scratched by fingernail, but can be scratched by copper coin.

Color: White, colorless. Fracture: Even.

Specific Gravity: 1.7 (light).

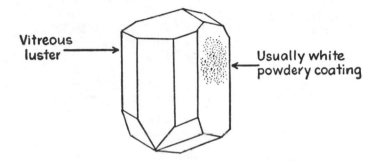

Vitreous luster →

← Usually white powdery coating

A hydrous sodium borate ($Na_2B_4O_7.10H_2O$), borax is a mineral having an old Arabic name. In 1856 it had been discovered at Borax Lake, Calif., and large crystals were removed from the mud at the bottom of the lake. Later, borax supplied the famous Death Valley twenty-mule teams with the useful product also called borax, which is employed in a hundred industries. From Furnace Creek and Resting Springs they hauled it to the railroad at Mojave. Searles Lake is now the world's largest deposit, one of astonishing volume. Around the borax lakes in California, and similarly in Tibet, the mineral is found to have crystallized on the shore. Some of the American deposits are situated in Nevada. Borax is also obtained from hot springs and brines in northern Italy. The dyed-in-the-wool mineral enthusiast who enjoys licking samples to see them shine would find that borax has a slightly sweetish yet alkaline taste. It is soluble in water and turns to chalky white tincalconite in a dry atmosphere.

135

APATITE

KEYS: Nonmetallic luster. Leaves white mark or scratch on streak plate. Does not show good cleavage. Cannot be scratched by copper coin, but can be scratched by knife blade.

Color: Green, brown. Fracture: Even.

Specific Gravity: 3.1–3.2 (medium weight).

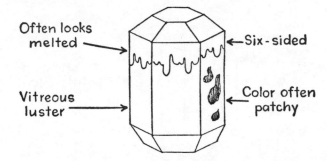

Often looks melted

Six-sided

Vitreous luster

Color often patchy

Apatite is calcium phosphate with the formula $Ca_5(PO_4)_3(F,Cl,OH)$. This intriguing name has nothing to do with food but comes from a Greek word meaning "to deceive," because of the resemblance to other minerals. Still, apatite does relate to food, in that it is a constituent of tooth enamel. No other crystals of apatite have ever exceeded in quality those found at Knappenwand in Austria, where they are complexly formed and wonderfully limpid. The largest apatite deposit is situated on the Kola Peninsula in the Soviet Union, where it is mined for fertilizer on account of its phosphate content. Substantial amounts occur along the southern coast of Norway. The clear greenish-yellow crystals from Mexico are appropriately called asparagus stone. The many excellent specimens from New England include purple crystals from Maine and dark-greenish and blue ones from Connecticut. A single crystal weighing over 550 pounds was found in Buckingham Township, Que. The luster of apatite has almost a resinous look.

PYROMORPHITE

KEYS: Nonmetallic luster. Leaves white mark or scratch on streak plate. Does not show good cleavage. Cannot be scratched by copper coin, but can be scratched by knife blade.

Color: Green. Fracture: Even.

Specific Gravity: 6.5–7.1 (very heavy).

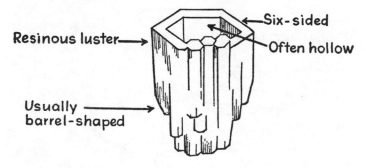

Resinous luster⟶ ⟵Six-sided

⟵Often hollow

Usually ⟶ barrel-shaped

Phosphate of lead and chlorine [$Pb_5Cl(PO_4)_3$], pyromorphite is the most prominent member of a series of minerals which closely resemble one another in composition. With a substitution of arsenic for phosphorus, pyromorphite grades into mimetite; the crystals of both are similar to those of vanadinite, and all these minerals have a fairly wide range of shades besides the most typical colors stated here as their properties. Not only do the crystals of pyromorphite occur in hollow barrel-shaped forms, but they also grow in parallel six-sided tubes which expand upward from a slender point. Some of the finest crystals are the violet and brown ones from Poullaouen and Huelgoat, France. Good specimens have come from Phoenixville, Pa.; Friedrichssegen, Germany; and Horcajo, Spain. Pyromorphite is a lesser ore of lead, and it occurs with other lead minerals in the upper levels of mines. The name is derived from Greek words meaning "fire" and "form," because a melted drop acquires a crystalline shape when it cools.

WILLEMITE

KEYS: Nonmetallic luster. Leaves white mark or scratch on streak plate. Does not show good cleavage. Cannot be scratched by copper coin, but can be scratched by knife blade.

Color: Yellowish-green, brown. Fracture: Uneven.

Specific Gravity: 3.9–4.2 (heavy).

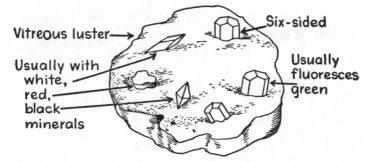

Vitreous luster→

Six-sided

Usually with white, red, black minerals

Usually fluoresces green

Willemite, zinc silicate (Zn_2SiO_4), is a valuable ore of zinc at Franklin, N.J., where its intimate association with black franklinite, red zincite, and white calcite makes one of the most distinctive combinations of minerals known anywhere. Willemite is white when pure, but its normal colors are yellowish-green and reddish-brown. Slender crystals of a delicate apple-green color, and larger flesh-red crystals containing manganese and known as troostite also occur in New Jersey. The glowing fluorescence of two of the minerals from this extraordinary locality—willemite appearing green and calcite rose-red—constitutes a striking feature of the mineral assemblage. Because of it the willemite can be hand-picked from conveyer belts moving under an ultraviolet light. Willemite has also been found in a few isolated localities in the western part of the United States; at Altenberg, Belgium; Musartut, Greenland; and several places in Africa. It was named after King William I of the Netherlands (Willem Frederik, who reigned from 1815 to 1840).

138

WULFENITE

KEYS: Nonmetallic luster. Leaves white mark or scratch on streak plate. Does not show good cleavage. Cannot be scratched by copper coin, but can be scratched by knife blade.
Color: Yellow. Fracture: Even.
Specific Gravity: 6.3–7.0 (very heavy).

Resinous luster⟶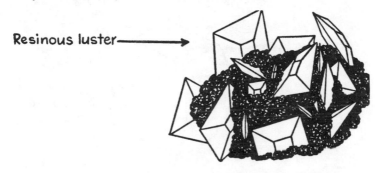

Wulfenite, which is a lead molybdate ($PbMoO_4$), is only to a small extent an ore of molybdenum, but its crystals are some of the loveliest in the mineral kingdom. Some of them, resembling wafers of butterscotch candy, look tasty enough to be eaten. The orange-red tabular crystals from the Hamburg and Red Cloud mines in Yuma County, Ariz., are as much as 2 inches long. Paper-thin crystals of good size come from Box Elder County, Utah; and a dozen other localities in the Western states of Nevada, New Mexico, Arizona, and Utah have produced superior crystals grouped at various angles like the disarranged compartment of a candy box. The color runs from a brilliant red to orange, yellow, and brown and at times may be green or gray. Specimens from the Sierra de los Lamentos, Mexico, grace many a collector's cabinet. This mineral was named in 1845 for Franz Xaver von Wulfen (1728–1805), an Austrian Jesuit priest and mineralogist. It usually results from the decomposition of other minerals. Its associates are vanadinite and pyromorphite.

SPHENE

KEYS: Nonmetallic luster. Leaves white mark or scratch on streak plate. Does not show good cleavage. Cannot be scratched by copper coin, but can be scratched by knife blade.

Color: Greenish-yellow, brown. Fracture: Conchoidal.

Specific Gravity: 3.4–3.5 (medium weight).

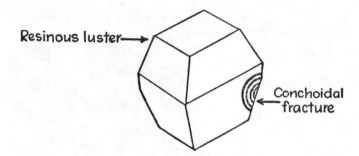

Resinous luster⟶

Conchoidal ⟵fracture

A silicate of calcium and titanium ($CaTiSiO_5$), sphene owes its name to the wedge-shaped crystals in which it often grows. An equally familiar name is titanite, indicating its chemical composition. Large crystals, darker in color than average, are found in a number of places in New York, Ontario, and Quebec. Those from Diana, N.Y., and Eganville, Ont., are dark-brown; those from Litchfield, Que., are shiny-black. Some of the broad reddish crystals from the Ala Valley in Italy are exceptionally attractive. Numerous places in Switzerland yield good crystals of sphene, including the large pale-green twins occurring at Saint Gotthard. The Kola Peninsula of Russia, between the Arctic Ocean and the White Sea, contains the largest deposit, used there as an ore of titanium. Transparent sphene, though not overly abundant, makes spectacular gems because of its superior luster and light-refracting power, but its softness hinders its use in jewelry. Sphene is common in granite but as an accessory to the more essential minerals.

SCHEELITE

KEYS: Nonmetallic luster. Leaves white mark or scratch on streak plate. Does not show good cleavage. Cannot be scratched by copper coin, but can be scratched by knife blade.

Color: White, gray. Fracture: Even.

Specific Gravity: 5.9–6.1 (heavy).

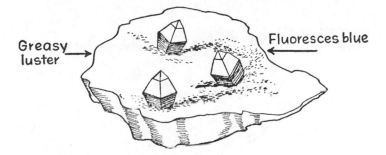

Greasy luster → ← Fluoresces blue

Calcium tungstate ($CaWO_4$) is scheelite. Although other ores yield more of the world's supply of tungsten, scheelite is the most important American source. It is one of the few minerals that can almost always be relied upon to fluoresce in ultraviolet light, the ensuing color being a bright bluish-white. As molybdenum replaces some of the atoms of tungsten, scheelite grades toward another mineral, powellite, and the fluorescence becomes white and then yellowish. Mineral collectors using short-wave ultraviolet lamps have come across numerous small occurrences of both minerals during the past decade. Scheelite was named in honor of Karl Wilhelm Scheele (1742–1786), the Swedish chemist who discovered in it the element tungsten, now called wolfram. Crystals of scheelite are not common; Traversella, Italy, and Framont, France, are noteworthy localities for them, and some of considerable size have been found in the tin mines of Germany, Czechoslovakia, and England. Large deposits of scheelite occur near Mill City, Nev., and Bishop and Atolia, Calif.

DATOLITE

KEYS: Nonmetallic luster. Leaves white mark or scratch on streak plate. Does not show good cleavage. Cannot be scratched by copper coin, but can be scratched by knife blade.
Color: Colorless, white, light-green.
Fracture: Conchoidal.
Specific Gravity: 2.9–3.0 (medium weight).

Vitreous luster

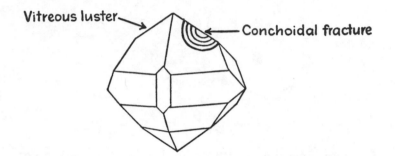

Conchoidal fracture

A basic silicate of calcium and boron [CaBSiO$_4$ (OH)], datolite is a mineral of secondary origin, forming in cavities in lava rock, such as basalt. It is associated with the zeolite minerals. Its occurrences are in regions where volcanic rock is abundant; for instance, in New Jersey and the Connecticut River Valley in the United States, and in the Harz Mountains of Germany. Datolite is one of the characteristic minerals in the Michigan copper deposits around Lake Superior, where, in addition to fine crystals having a greenish tinge, cream-colored and pinkish porcelainlike masses are found which contain inclusions of native copper and are sometimes polished as gem material. Italy and Norway are other leading countries for specimens of datolite. The complex crystals, usually of pale-green tint, have many faces distributed at odd angles over the surface. Otherwise this mineral is difficult to recognize without chemical tests.

ARAGONITE

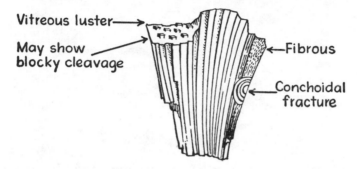

Vitreous luster⟶

May show blocky cleavage

⟵Fibrous

Conchoidal fracture

Aragonite is calcium carbonate $(CaCO_3)$. It thus has the same chemical composition as calcite, and, like all carbonates, it fizzes in acid. Although less common than calcite, aragonite is formed under various conditions ranging from the hot water of geysers to the cold water of the ocean. It also forms as a crust inside of teakettles and water tanks. Named in 1796 from its original locality in the former kingdom of Aragón, Spain, this interesting mineral has been found in almost every country. Some collectors like best the six-sided disks known in Wyoming and Colorado as "Indian dollars" and in New Mexico as "Aztec money." Some of these are twin crystals which have changed over to calcite. Other collectors prefer the twisting branches that resemble snow-white coral and are known as "flos ferri." Large, well-formed crystals of aragonite occur in the sulfur deposits on the island of Sicily. The upper part of many coral reefs in the Pacific Ocean consists of aragonite, as does the mother-of-pearl of oyster and abalone shells.

ANALCIME

KEYS: Nonmetallic luster. Leaves white mark or scratch on streak plate. Does not show good cleavage. Cannot be scratched by copper coin, but can be scratched by knife blade.
Color: Colorless, white. Fracture: Even.
Specific Gravity: 2.2–2.4 (medium weight).

Vitreous luster⟶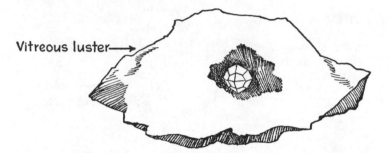

Analcime is a hydrous silicate of sodium and aluminum ($NaAlSiO_6.H_2O$). It is one of the most important members of the zeolite family, all of which boil up, giving off water evenly when heated. The word zeolite, in fact, comes from the Greek word meaning "to boil." The beautiful glassy crystals of analcime in the Cyclopean Islands in the Mediterranean Sea are typical of how this mineral occurs in cavities in volcanic rock. Large white crystals are found on the Seiser Alp, Italy. Some giant crystals of analcime measure a foot in diameter. Among many other localities are those on isolated Kerguelen Island in the Indian Ocean; at Cape Blomidon, Nova Scotia; North Table Mountain, overlooking Golden, Colo.; Bergen Hill, N.J.; and in the Lake Superior copper district. Analcime, also written analcite, has the same appearance as leucite and white garnet; unlike leucite, it grows in rock cavities, and it is softer than garnet. Analcime was named in 1797 from the Greek word for "weak" because of its feeble electrical nature.

144

MAGNESITE

KEYS: Nonmetallic luster. Leaves white mark or scratch on streak plate. Does not show good cleavage. Cannot be scratched by copper coin, but can be scratched by knife blade.

Color: Green. Fracture: Conchoidal.
Specific Gravity: 2.9–3.1 (medium weight).

Vitreous luster

Porcelainlike

Conchoidal fracture

Often rhombic cleavage

As its name suggests, magnesite is magnesium carbonate ($MgCO_3$). It, like the rest of the carbonates, fizzes in acid, which should be warmed for best results. Magnesite is used to make bricks for lining metallurgical furnaces, and it has served as an ore of magnesium metal, now extracted mostly from sea water. Large clear crystals occur at Bom Jesús dos Meiras, Brazil. Some of the rare prismatic crystals are found at Orangedale, Nova Scotia. Sizable deposits of commercial magnesite are situated at Chewelah, Wash.; bordering both the Coast Ranges and the Sierra Nevada in California; and in the Paradise Range in Nevada. Abroad they are especially large in Manchuria, the Ural Mountains, and Austria. A classic locality is the island of Euboea, Greece. Magnesite is slightly harder than calcite, and when occurring in cleavable masses it may require a chemical test for magnesium to distinguish it from calcite. At times the usual porcelainlike compact varieties give the impression of being harder and tougher than they are.

OLIVINE

KEYS: Nonmetallic luster. Leaves white mark or scratch on streak plate. Does not show good cleavage. Can scratch glass and be scratched by quartz.

Color: Green. Fracture: Conchoidal.

Specific Gravity: 3.3–3.4 (medium weight).

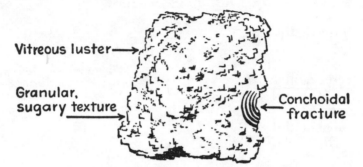

Vitreous luster→

Granular, sugary texture

Conchoidal fracture

This magnesium-iron silicate $[(Mg,Fe)_2SiO_4]$ was so named because of its olive-green color. With its tendency to form separate grains, a specimen may resemble somewhat a bowl of nearly round pale olives much shrunken in size. Olivine is a member of a mineral series grading from forsterite to fayalite. When transparent and having a distinctive bottle-green shade, olivine is fashioned into gems called peridot. St. John's Island in the Red Sea is the most celebrated locality for peridot, and rounded grains may be secured on some of the Indian reservations in the American Southwest. Common olivine is abundant in many dark and heavy rocks, those formed deep in the earth's crust. The rocks called dunite and peridotite are composed entirely or mostly of olivine. Volcanic bombs are often solid masses of olivine, and crystals of olivine are found in the lava which has flowed from Mount Vesuvius. Olivine is the most typical mineral in nonmetallic meteorites. The largest known crystals, from Snarum, Norway, have almost completely altered to serpentine.

146

IDOCRASE

KEYS: Nonmetallic luster. Leaves white mark or scratch on streak plate. Does not show good cleavage. Can scratch glass and be scratched by quartz.

Color: Green, brown. Fracture: Uneven.
Specific Gravity: 3.4 (medium weight).

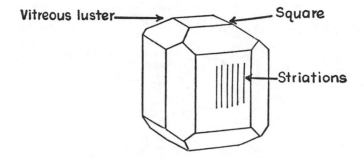

Vitreous luster —→ Square

Striations

A complex silicate of aluminum, idocrase is also known by its older name, vesuvianite, which indicates one of its first known localities, Mount Vesuvius, where sparkling brown crystals occur. A compact green variety with whitish streaks, resembling jade, is called californite; it is found in Siskiyou, Fresno, and Tulare Counties, Calif. Other localities in the United States include those situated in Arkansas, Maine, Vermont, New Jersey, and New York. In Quebec large brownish-yellow crystals of idocrase occur at Calumet Falls, while at Templeton the crystals are brownish-red. The clearest and best-formed crystals are the transparent green and brown ones from Ala, Italy. Large brown crystals come from Egg, near Kristiansand, Norway. Idocrase originates as a result of the action of heated rocks on beds of limestone, which may be changed to marble with segregations of idocrase and other minerals, such as garnet and diopside. Besides the californite variety, clear specimens of idocrase have been used as gem stones; a superior locality for them is Eden, Vt.

TURQUOISE

KEYS: Nonmetallic luster. Leaves white mark or scratch on streak plate. Does not show good cleavage. Can scratch glass and be scratched by quartz.

Color: Blue, green. Fracture: Conchoidal.

Specific Gravity: 2.6–2.8 (medium weight).

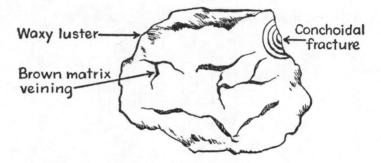

Waxy luster

Conchoidal fracture

Brown matrix veining

Turquoise, a hydrous aluminum phosphate [CuAl$_6$-(PO$_4$)$_4$(OH)$_8$.4H$_2$O], is one of the minerals most favored as a gem since prehistoric times. Ancient mines in Egypt and Persia produced it many centuries ago, and the Persian deposits near Nishapur are still productive. The material they yield is accepted as the standard of quality for choice blue stones containing a minimum of iron-colored matrix. When the matrix, or adjoining rock. is present as a delicate veining, it creates the delightful spider-web pattern, desired by many buyers as a sign of genuineness. Turquoise reaches its peak of popularity with the American Indian, to whom it holds a good deal of symbolism as well as beauty. The once extensive deposits near Santa Fe, New Mexico, are largely depleted, the leading ones now being in Nevada and Colorado. The mineral usually occurs in stringers and small nodules. Large pieces of turquoise have been found recently in copper mines in Arizona. The word turquoise is French for "Turkish," the Persian stones having reached Europe by way of Turkey.

148

PREHNITE

KEYS: Nonmetallic luster. Leaves white mark or scratch on streak plate. Does not show good cleavage. Can scratch glass and be scratched by quartz.
Color: Light-green. Fracture: Uneven.
Specific Gravity: 2.8–3.0 (medium weight).

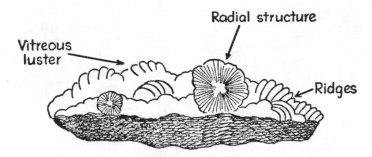

Radial structure

Vitreous luster

Ridges

A hydrous aluminum silicate $[Ca_2Al_2Si_3O_{10}(OH)_2]$, prehnite was named in 1790 in recognition of Col. von Prehn, who brought the first specimen to Europe from South Africa. It resembles the zeolite minerals in some respects and occurs with them in cavities in volcanic rocks. First-rate crystals are found at Coopersburg, Pa., but elsewhere prehnite grows mostly in jug-shaped or rounded aggregates, in which the individual rectangular plates of the cockscomb structure are scarcely noticeable except upon close examination. Prehnite looks like hemimorphite, which is, however, far more resistant to heat; although prehnite fuses easily, it does not give off water quite so readily. Interesting barrel-shaped groups, enclosed in white asbestos, have been found near Bourg d'Oisans, France. Leading localities in America for prehnite are Farmington, Conn.; Somerville, Mass.; the New Jersey trap quarries; and the Michigan copper region. Localities in other countries include the Kilpatrick Hills in Scotland, and Cradock, Union of South Africa, from where the original material came.

149

LEUCITE

KEYS: Nonmetallic luster. Leaves white mark or scratch on streak plate. Does not show good cleavage. Can scratch glass and be scratched by quartz.

Color: White, gray. Fracture: Conchoidal.

Specific Gravity: 2.5 (medium weight).

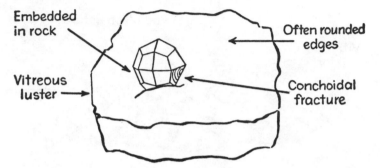

Leucite is a potassium–aluminum silicate ($KAlSi_2O_6$) and was named because of its color; it is often called white garnet, which it resembles. Like sodalite, leucite belongs to the feldspathoid group of minerals. It originates at high temperatures in lava rocks. The best crystals are from Mount Vesuvius, where small clear crystals fall like hailstones during eruptions and large perfect crystals are found in the big blocks of rock thrown out by the violence of the explosion. Magnificent groups of leucite crystals have been picked up as drift boulders on the shore of Vancouver Island, B.C. The Leucite Hills in Wyoming contain this mineral in abundance, and so do some of the mountains in Montana—the Bear Paw and Highwood Mountains, for example—but otherwise leucite is rare in the United States. It can be distinguished from garnet by its being softer and from analcime, another similar-looking mineral, by its favoring solid rock in which to grow, rather than cavities. Leucite is not too stable a mineral, converting to white or gray alteration products from its naturally colorless state.

QUARTZ

KEYS: Nonmetallic luster. Leaves white mark or scratch on streak plate. Does not show good cleavage. Can scratch glass and be scratched by quartz.

Color: Colorless, white, gray, black.
Fracture: Conchoidal.
Specific Gravity: 2.7 (medium weight).

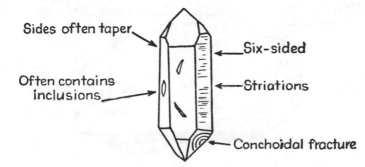

Although an oxide of silicon (SiO_2) in chemical composition, quartz is now considered a sort of parent of the enormous number of silicate minerals, inasmuch as its atomic structure is similar to them. So numerous are the varieties of quartz that they occur in every color and a fantastic array of patterns. Rock crystal—such as fortune-tellers use for spheres, scientists use for controlling frequency in electronic devices, and the rest of us use for jewelry—is colorless quartz. Smoky quartz, as from the Alps, is richly brown or hazily black. Cairngorm, the national gem of Scotland, looks as topaz is popularly supposed to look. Rose quartz has a pink color, generally not lasting. Tiger's-eye, from Griqualand West, South Africa, is a blue asbestos turned to golden quartz. The most desired kind of quartz is amethyst, its choicest crystals a delectable purple or violet. The gem varieties of quartz are perhaps found most conspicuously in Brazil, Madagascar, and the United States.

CHALCEDONY

KEYS: Nonmetallic luster. Leaves white mark or scratch on streak plate. Does not show good cleavage. Can scratch glass and be scratched by quartz.

Color: Brown, green, gray, black, white.
Fracture: Conchoidal.
Specific Gravity: 2.6 (medium weight).

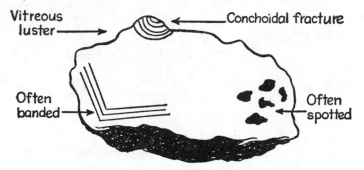

The atomic structure of certain varieties of quartz is so minutely developed that they are never able to mature as actual crystals with definite outward shapes. Many mineralogists classify them as belonging to a different mineral, called chalcedony. Some of the kinds of chalcedony are fibrous, while others are granular, but names are applied to them according to their colors and patterns, of which there are many. Agate, for instance, is a banded chalcedony, though moss agate reveals fernlike designs. Onyx is likewise banded, the layers being straight. Carnelian is red chalcedony; sard is brown; chrysoprase is green; bloodstone is also green but with red spots resembling drops of blood. Jasper occurs in many colors, typically dark-red, green, or yellowish-brown. Flint is the gray or black chalcedony used for implements by primitive man. Every part of the world furnishes these varieties for gem use, and they are the favorite stones of the thousands of amateur lapidaries who have a rewarding hobby in cutting and polishing them.

OPAL

KEYS: Nonmetallic luster. Leaves white mark or scratch on streak plate. Does not show good cleavage. Can scratch glass and be scratched by quartz.

Color: White. Fracture: Conchoidal.

Specific Gravity: 1.9–2.3 (light).

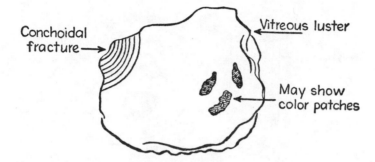

Conchoidal fracture

Vitreous luster

May show color patches

When water is present in a chalcedony-like substance, the material is hydrous silica $(SiO_2.nH_2O)$, called opal. This is one of the few minerals not having a definite atomic structure and never occurring in crystal form. Its varying appearance seems to reflect this inconstancy. Many lovers of fine gems regard opal as their favorite. Lacking any color of its own except as a background, it reveals all the hues of the rainbow in ever-changing, purest aspect. White opal, also called Hungarian opal, has a pale or white background. Black opal has a background which is usually dark-blue or gray, against which the colors flash. Australia is the true home of black opal, first discovered in 1905 at Lightning Ridge, New South Wales. Some of it is also produced from time to time in Humboldt County, Nev., but is apt to crack after exposure. The reddish fire opal from Querétaro, Mexico, is occasionally quite attractive. Mineral collectors, however, are likely to find only the so-called common opal, which does not show the distinctive play of colors. Opalized wood is abundant in western United States.

153

TOURMALINE

KEYS: Nonmetallic luster. Leaves white mark or scratch on streak plate. Does not show good cleavage. Cannot be scratched by quartz.
Color: Black, pink, green. Fracture: Conchoidal.
Specific Gravity: 2.9–3.2 (medium weight).

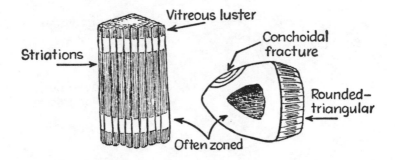

Tourmaline is an aluminum silicate with a formula so complex that John Ruskin said, "The chemistry of it is more like a medieval doctor's prescription than the making of a respectable mineral." It occurs in a tremendously wide range of colors. More than that, the colors are often zones either along the length or across the width of the unique rounded-triangular crystals. Watermelon tourmaline, for example, has a green exterior, surrounding first a white zone and then a red core. Each of the colors of tourmaline has a different name—rubellite, indicolite, achroite, dravite are some of them—but they are still tourmaline and eminently suited for use as gems. The jet-black specimens, which resemble hornblende, tend to fracture like coal. Pierrepont Manor, N.Y., is a renowned locality for black tourmaline. The more colorful varieties are especially noteworthy in the United States at Pala, Calif., and at Auburn and Paris, Me. The most prominent localities abroad are situated in Brazil, the Ural Mountains, and the islands of Ceylon, Madagascar, and Elba.

STAUROLITE

KEYS: Nonmetallic luster. Leaves white mark or scratch on streak plate. Does not show good cleavage. Cannot be scratched by quartz.

Color: Brown. Fracture. Conchoidal.

Specific Gravity: 3.7 (medium weight).

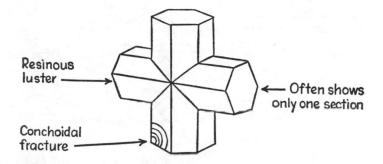

Resinous luster

Often shows only one section

Conchoidal fracture

Staurolite is an iron-aluminum silicate [$Fe(OH)Al_4 (AlSi_2) O_{12}$]. Although twin crystals have already been described for a number of minerals, staurolite is the one mineral above all others whose twins are of outstanding interest. Penetrating each other to form a Greek cross, to which staurolite owes its name, they are widely collected and kept as amulets. Called fairy crosses and figuring in local legends, those from Georgia and Virginia are eagerly sought, some being almost as smooth as though they had been polished. Rougher ones come from Cherokee County, N.C., and near Taos, N.M. The original localities for these crosses are in western France; large ones come from there and from Scotland. When the twin crystals of staurolite do not make a cross, they are shaped like the letter X instead. Single brown crystals of staurolite—lustrous and translucent—are found on Monte Campione, Switzerland. Fine crystals occur at Chesterfield, Mass. The untwinned crystals bear a resemblance to andalusite, which, however, is nearly square in outline.

ZIRCON

KEYS: Nonmetallic luster. Leaves white mark or scratch on streak plate. Does not show good cleavage. Cannot be scratched by quartz.

Color: Brown. **Fracture:** Uneven.

Specific Gravity: 4.7 (heavy).

Adamantine luster

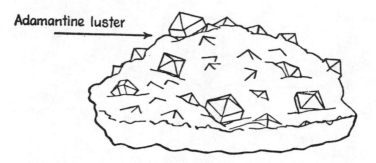

This is a silicate of the metal zirconium ($ZrSiO_4$). The name zircon has an obscure origin dating back many centuries. The metal was named from the mineral, which has been known since ancient times as one of the more remarkable of the gem stones. Three structural types have been proved to exist; these are termed high, intermediate, and low zircon. Several beautiful colors are available, including blue and golden yellow, as well as colorless stones which resemble diamonds. Those that are some shade of orange are called hyacinth and jacinth. These have almost all been heat-treated to produce the desired hue. Deep-red and mysterious green zircons are entirely natural. The gemmy crystals are found mostly in Ceylon and Indo-China. In Canada large crystals of ordinary zircon come from Sebastopol, Ont., and Templeton Township, Que. In Madagascar they are numerous on Mount Ampanobe. Exquisite tiny zircon crystals accumulate in beach sands in North Carolina, Florida, and elsewhere, for they have washed out of granite and similar rocks, in which they are a frequent constituent.

ANDALUSITE

KEYS: Nonmetallic luster. Leaves white mark or scratch on streak plate. Does not show good cleavage. Cannot be scratched by quartz.

Color: Gray, brown. Fracture: Uneven.

Specific Gravity: 3.1–3.2 (medium weight).

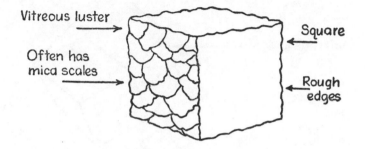

Vitreous luster →

Often has mica scales →

← Square

← Rough edges

Andalusite (named after the province of Andalusia in Spain) is an aluminum silicate with the same chemical formula as kyanite and sillimanite (Al_2SiO_5). When heated, it becomes mullite, which is the porcelain used in making spark plugs. The variety known as chiastolite has inside a dark cross of organic matter, which assumes different shapes as the crystal is sliced—sometimes appearing as a wedge, sometimes as an hourglass. The large specimens of chiastolite from Rohan, France, are outstanding, as are those from the Lisenser Alp in the Austrian Tirol. Superior crystals are also found at Bimbourie, South Australia. Gem-quality andalusite is not common and is remarkable for the fact that the cut stones appear either olive-green or blood-red, according to how they are held. Stream-worn pebbles of this quality come from Brazil. The mineral is mined in commercial quantities near Laws, Calif. Good specimens come from Maine, Pennsylvania, and several places in Massachusetts; the stout crystals often project as knots from the rock. Andalusite-rich sand occurs in South Africa.

GARNET

KEYS: Nonmetallic luster. Leaves white mark or scratch on streak plate. Does not show good cleavage. Cannot be scratched by quartz.

Color: Red, brown, yellow, green, black, white.
Fracture: Even. Specific Gravity: 3.5–4.3 (heavy).

Vitreous luster⟶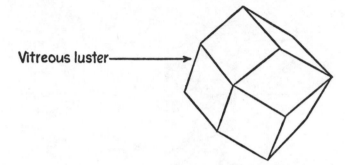

Garnet is a group of minerals which are silicates of aluminum, calcium, and other elements. The various garnets closely resemble one another, and even their colors usually give no assurance as to their individual identity. They are often recognized most readily by the other minerals associated with them, because each of the different garnets has its own type of geologic occurrence. Almandite, as mined in heavy crystals in eastern New York, is an important abrasive. When transparent and deep-red, this kind of garnet is known as precious garnet. Pyrope, the familiar dark-red Bohemian garnet in grandmother's jewelry, is also called precious garnet. Rhodolite is a lovely rose-colored garnet from North Carolina, corresponding to two parts of pyrope and one of almandite. Spessartite is brown or red and occurs in light-colored igneous rock. Grossularite includes white crystals, as well as those of more usual colors. Uvarovite is always green. Unsurpassed among all the gem garnets, however, is demantoid, a brilliant green variety of andradite from the Ural Mountains, used as a substitute for emerald.

BERYL

KEYS: Nonmetallic luster. Leaves white mark or scratch on streak plate. Does not show good cleavage. Cannot be scratched by quartz.

Color: Bluish-green, light-yellow, white.

Fracture: Conchoidal.

Specific Gravity: 2.6–2.8 (medium weight).

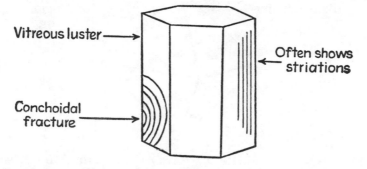

Beryl is a silicate of two light metals, beryllium and aluminum [$Be_3Al_2(SiO_3)_6$]. From it is extracted the strategic metal beryllium, which was named after it. Beryl, furthermore, is one of the major gem stones. When green, it is emerald; when blue or bluish-green, it is aquamarine; when pink, it is morganite—all gems of exceptional loveliness. The emeralds from Muzo, Colombia, have been the model of quality since the middle of the sixteenth century. The other beryl gems are obtained most abundantly in Brazil, Madagascar, Siberia, Ceylon, and California. Pretty aquamarine crystals are found at the very summit of 14,245-foot Mount Antero, Colo., the highest mineral locality in North America. Common beryl, used industrially, may occur in huge rough crystals, such as the two weighing 25 and 18 tons which were uncovered at Albany, Me., and the 40-ton monster reported from Madagascar. Another, with a weight of 3,000 pounds, came from Grafton, N.H. Aquamarine crystals often weigh several hundred pounds.

SPINEL

KEYS: Nonmetallic luster. Leaves white mark or scratch on streak plate. Does not show good cleavage. Cannot be scratched by quartz.

Color: Black, brown, green, pink. Fracture: Conchoidal.
Specific Gravity: 3.6 (medium weight).

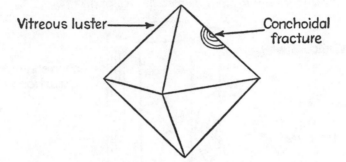

Vitreous luster ⟶   Conchoidal fracture

Magnesium aluminate ($MgAl_2O_4$) in natural form is spinel. An anciently known mineral, carrying a name whose origin was lost in the distant past, spinel furnishes gems in a considerable range of colors which resemble those of other gems, especially ruby and sapphire. The Black Prince's ruby, one of the most historic stones among the British crown jewels, has been proved to be actually spinel. Owing to its hardness, spinel is found as rolled pebbles in placer sand in the gem fields of Ceylon and Burma, together with the corundum which looks so much like it. Crystals of ordinary spinel, colored green, brown, and black, are distributed in a belt of rock extending from Andover, N.J., to Amity, N.Y.; and including a number of established collecting localities. Large crystals are found at Ambatomainty, Madagascar. Spinel crystals are like those of diamond and magnetite but are not so hard as diamond and are not magnetic like magnetite. Gahnite, often called zinc spinel, is a similar mineral found in many places; crystals 5 inches across have been acquired at Franklin, N.J.

CHAPTER 5

Four Keys to Recognizing Rocks

ROCK KEY NO. 1   TEXTURE AND STRUCTURE

The size, shape, and pattern of the mineral grains in a rock are included in the term *texture*. The larger features of rocks, as seen in the field, are called *structures*, but in specimens of the size that can be conveniently held in one's hand there is scarcely any difference between texture and structure as they are often observed.

Nothing indicates better than its texture the conditions under which a rock has been formed. If the rock is igneous, the texture may tell whether intrusive or extrusive; if sedimentary, it tells whether it is an accumulation or a precipitate; if metamorphic, it tells what changes the original rock has undergone.

One of the most significant aspects of rock texture depends upon whether the individual particles can be seen by the unaided eye. Since even the smallest grain becomes visible when you examine it closely, this statement really refers to whether the separate minerals are large enough to be recognized by name, as in typical granite, without having to be magnified with a lens.

Some igneous rocks contain holes left by the escape of gas from the lava while it cooled. Pumice is an ideal example. This sort of porous texture or structure can be useful in recognizing certain extrusive rocks.

The structure of many rocks is layered or banded. This may mean successive deposits of sediment, each laid on top of the older ones, as in sandstone. Or it may show repeated flows of lava, or the streaked effect that cooling magma sometimes gives. Or it may be proof of metamorphism, which squeezes and stretches the minerals until they take on a ribboned appearance, as in gneiss.

Until you are able to recognize the origin of an unknown rock—this skill will come with practice in collecting rocks and reading about them—you can at least determine whether it can be split into layers with a prospector's pick. This experiment classifies the rock as either cleavable or not cleavable.

ROCK KEY NO. 2   COLOR

Color is even less reliable a guide to the identity of rocks than it is for minerals, for the obvious reason that most rocks are composed of several different minerals, each of which may have a quite different color. When the size of the individual mineral grains is small, however, a rock may present an over-all color easy to describe and compare.

Just as marble ranges from snow-white to jet-black, so many other rocks also occur in a variety of colors. Those colors, however, which are fairly characteristic of certain rocks are used in the outline and descriptive section for the purpose of helping you to name them as readily as possible.

Light-colored igneous rocks such as granite tend to be lighter in weight, that is, have a lower specific gravity, than dark-colored ones. This is because the iron that so often makes rocks dark also makes them heavy. In the outline and descriptive section, therefore, color and weight are given together. The relationship is not always dependable, though, because some lightweight specimens are dark as a result of structural peculiarities; obsidian, for example, has the chemical composition of granite and weighs even less, but it is often black because of tiny dust-like specks which absorb the light.

ROCK KEY NO. 3   ACID TEST

The carbonate rocks, such as limestone and marble, will fizz, or effervesce, when touched with acid, owing to the evolution of carbon dioxide gas. A good idea is to gouge the rock with a knife blade, producing a powder which dissolves more rapidly than the solid rock. Any acid may be used, but ordinary household vinegar will do.

162

Many igneous rocks, especially those from ore deposits, have veins of calcite or some other carbonate mineral in them and appear to effervesce vigorously. The action is confined to certain places and soon ceases, however, whereas a true carbonate rock will continue to fizz all over for a long time if enough acid is applied.

Pieces of carbonate minerals and rocks may similarly be present in a sedimentary rock, such as conglomerate or sandstone. These should not be confused with the bulk of the rock, which may scarcely react at all. Even more deceptive is the fizzing, often violent, of carbonate cement in a sedimentary rock, particularly sandstone. With such a rock it is necessary to wait and see whether the grains themselves are also dissolving or only the cementing material is being affected.

ROCK KEY NO. 4   MINERAL CONTENT

Rocks can best be named by recognizing their individual minerals where visible. This method requires a knowledge of the physical properties of minerals, as described in the previous section of this book. Because the mineral grains in rocks are generally so much smaller than when found as separate mineral specimens, a sample collection of good-sized pieces is worth buying for a few cents each from an established mineral dealer, so that you will become familiar with them and be able to recognize them when you meet them again in smaller grains in ordinary rocks.

Most rocks are named scientifically according to their mineral content. A simplified classification of this sort is used in this book as a secondary means of identifying the coarse-grained igneous rocks, in which the minerals are large enough to be recognized by anyone familiar with their appearance.

Identifying the Rocks. Outline of Keys

PORPHYRY

KEYS: Minerals easily seen with unaided eye. One kind of mineral set in finer-grained background.

Color: Variable. Acid Test: Does not fizz in acid.

Mineral Content: Variable.

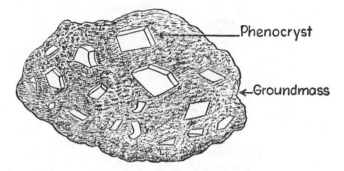

The term porphyry is used for igneous rocks that exhibit individual grains or crystals of a mineral set "like plums in a pudding" against a general background of finer texture. The background is called the groundmass, and the larger grains—the "plums"—are called phenocrysts. As long as there is a distinct difference in size between the two parts of the pattern, either can be of any degree of coarseness. For instance, the groundmass may consist of grains so tiny that it appears to have a uniform surface, and then the phenocrysts need only be large enough to be separately visible. Or the groundmass may be as coarse as granite, in which case the phenocrysts will have to be of substantial size, each perhaps several inches or more across. Porphyry is thus a descriptive term, including rocks of quite different composition. Thus, there are granite porphyry, syenite porphyry, monzonite porphyry, gabbro porphyry, felsite porphyry, and basalt porphyry. Miners and prospectors in the American West, however, commonly use the term for almost any fine-grained rock found in dikes associated with ore deposits.

GNEISS

KEYS: **Minerals easily seen with unaided eye. Minerals in layers.**

Color: Variable. **Acid Test:** Does not fizz in acid.

Mineral Content: Feldspar, quartz, biotite, hornblende.

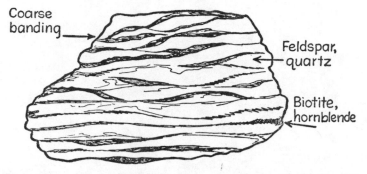

Coarse banding

Feldspar, quartz

Biotite, hornblende

Pronounced "nice," this rock is coarsely banded, the different layers of minerals being roughly parallel in a wide curving pattern. Dark and light bands occur in succession across the specimen, and each band may consist of several different layers. The minerals are predominantly feldspar and quartz, but biotite mica and hornblende are fairly abundant as well. Gneiss is a metamorphic rock created when either an igneous or a sedimentary rock is subjected to heat and enormous pressure. This causes it to be squeezed and stretched, pulling the minerals into stringers which occasionally narrow and widen along their length. An interesting variety is augen-gneiss, in which oval fragments of feldspar look like eyes peering out of the rock. As the bands become thinner, gneiss grades into another rock, called schist. Although it can be almost any age, gneiss is especially frequent in the older rocks, which have had full occasion to be buried deeply under thick layers of sediments and to be involved in the mountain-making processes. Fine examples of gneiss occur in the Highlands of Scotland, in Scandinavia, and in eastern Canada.

166

CONGLOMERATE

KEYS: Minerals easily seen with unaided eye. Minerals in layers.

Color: Variable. Acid Test: Does not fizz in acid.

Mineral Content: Quartz, feldspar, variable.

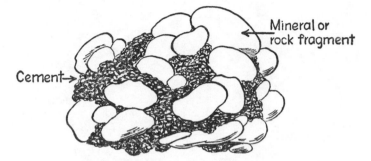

Mineral or rock fragment

Cement→

The individual fragments in the sedimentary rock called conglomerate may be the size of gravel, or as large as boulders, or a mixture of various coarse sizes larger than sand. A filling of sand generally occupies the spaces between them. The particles may consist of a single mineral, usually quartz or feldspar, or they may be a mixture of many minerals or pieces of rock. The cementing material between the grains, though mostly hardened sand, may also be clay, calcite, iron oxide, or silica. Puddingstone is a conglomerate which shows a distinct contrast between its large pebbles and the dense matrix in which they are enclosed. When the fragments have sharp corners, not well rounded by stream action, the rock is known as a breccia. Conglomerates otherwise are deposited mostly by water, though some are the result of glacial action. The most extensive example of this rock in the United States, formerly called the Great Conglomerate, lies underneath the coal beds in Pennsylvania and adjacent states. Another Great Conglomerate, in northern Michigan and Wisconsin, is 2,200 feet thick. Ancient conglomerates are widespread in Canada.

167

GRANITE

KEYS: Minerals easily seen with unaided eye. Minerals mutually intergrown. Light color; light weight.

Acid Test: Does not fizz in acid.

Mineral Content: Feldspar, quartz, biotite, hornblende.

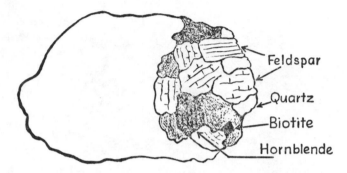

The igneous rock that consists of potash feldspar and quartz in readily visible grains of about equal size is called granite. Other minerals, especially plagioclase feldspar, biotite mica, and hornblende, may be present; but potash feldspar and quartz are essential, and they predominate. Granite should typically be a light-colored rock. It is true that the color is normally white or light gray, but when the feldspar is darker because of its structure, the rock is correspondingly dark. The well-known Quincy granite from Massachusetts is dark-gray, and even red granite, as it occurs so extensively in Minnesota and Scotland, is not uncommon. Though it may appear dark, granite is less heavy than the true dark rocks—the so-called "basic" rocks, such as gabbro—which are dark because of their prominent iron content. The cores of many of the world's great mountain ranges are composed of granite, and elsewhere it is deeply hidden. Granite is one of the major building and monument stones. A strikingly curious variety, called orbicular granite, is pock-marked with large knobs of the granite minerals.

168

PEGMATITE

KEYS: Minerals easily seen with unaided eye. Minerals mutually intergrown. Light color; light weight.

Acid Test: Does not fizz in acid.

Mineral Content: Feldspar, quartz, muscovite.

Extremely coarse igneous rock is called pegmatite, and the bodies themselves are spoken of as pegmatites. The minerals in the majority of specimens are perhaps twice as large as those in granite, but frequently they grow to gigantic sizes; the 47-foot spodumene in the Black Hills is the largest in America. Superlative crystals, unexcelled for perfection and beauty, as well as for size, are a feature of this kind of rock. The usual minerals in pegmatite are the same as those in granite—quartz and potash feldspar, mostly microcline. The mica is chiefly muscovite. A distinctive variety of pegmatite is graphic granite, so named because the grains of quartz and feldspar are intergrown in an angular fashion, so as to resemble ancient writing. Noted for their rare minerals as much as for their coarse texture, pegmatites are the home of fine gems and other minerals that are not found anywhere else. Rose quartz, smoky quartz, and moonstone are gems for which pegmatite is the main original source. Although the known masses of pegmatite may be of almost any shape, they are so commonly tabular that they are often referred to as pegmatite dikes.

SYENITE

KEYS: Minerals easily seen with unaided eye. Minerals mutually intergrown. Light color; light weight.

Acid Test: Does not fizz in acid.

Mineral Content: Feldspar, biotite, hornblende.

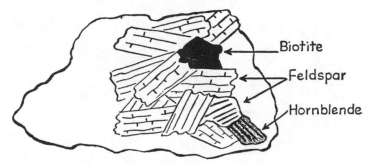

A rock very similar to granite in appearance but having little or no quartz is called syenite. The chief mineral is potash feldspar; in addition there is usually some plagioclase feldspar and a small amount of the dark minerals such as hornblende and biotite mica. The feldspar in syenite has a tendency to assume a rectangular shape. The name came from the old locality of Syene (now Aswân) in Egypt, which furnished a stone extensively used for obelisks in the times of the Pharaohs. The largest amount of syenite in the United States appears in the Adirondack Mountains, while other bodies are found in the White Mountains and the Rockies, and at the edge of the Ozark Mountains near Little Rock, Ark. In comparison with granite, however, syenite is relatively uncommon. Syenite serves the same commercial uses as granite, though it is more resistant to fire because of the absence of quartz. Larvikite is an exceptionally handsome syenite from Larvik, Norway, the feldspar of which shows a beautiful blue opalescence; this stone decorates the front of office buildings in New York and other cities in America and Europe.

MONZONITE

KEYS: Minerals easily seen with unaided eye. Minerals mutually intergrown. Light color; light weight.

Acid Test: Does not fizz in acid.

Mineral Content: Feldspar, biotite, hornblende, pyroxene.

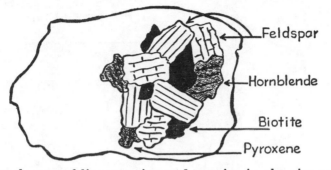

Closely resembling granite and syenite in the size and pattern of the minerals of which it is composed, monzonite is regarded as an intermediate igneous rock. When molten, it has less silica than molten granite; whatever amount was present has been taken up by the various silicate minerals, leaving little or none for the forming of quartz, which is pure silica. Having more iron than granite has, it contains more of the dark minerals, but not so many as gabbro, which has a still-higher content of iron. Hence monzonite stands between granite and gabbro in classification. Its essential minerals are about equal proportions of both kinds of feldspar—plagioclase and potash feldspar; the dark minerals present are biotite mica, hornblende, and augite. Since the two kinds of feldspar—usually so alike in appearance—are somewhat different in color when they occur together, monzonite is rather easily recognized by this fact of one being gray and the other white, or one white and the other pink. This is an important rock in connection with the metal-bearing mineral deposits in Colorado and elsewhere in western North America.

GABBRO

KEYS: Minerals easily seen with unaided eye. Minerals mutually intergrown. Dark color; heavy weight.

Acid Test: Does not fizz in acid.

Mineral Content: Feldspar, pyroxene, hornblende, olivine.

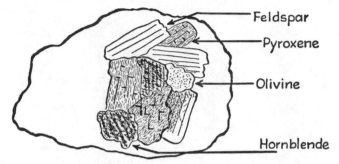

Feldspar

Pyroxene

Olivine

Hornblende

An igneous rock which is dark and heavy and which consists of plagioclase feldspar and other mineral grains large enough to be visible and recognized is called gabbro. The minerals are typically black, dark-gray, or dark-green in color, being chiefly plagioclase feldspar (mainly labradorite) and pyroxene (commonly augite), with some hornblende and olivine. When gabbro is composed almost exclusively of labradorite, the rock is called anorthosite, of which large amounts occur in Wyoming, eastern Canada, and Scandinavia. Another kind of gabbro, called norite, encloses huge deposits of nickel ore, especially at Sudbury, Ont., and chromium and platinum ore, as in South Africa. Gabbro is a deep-seated rock, formed at high temperatures. It is a familiar sight in the vicinity of Baltimore, Md.; at Duluth, Minn.; and elsewhere around Lake Superior; and in the Adirondack Mountains. Less popular than granite on account of its somber appearance, gabbro is easier to work; in Sweden it is favored for monuments and sculpture. When it decomposes, it yields a reddish soil because of the high content of iron in the dark minerals.

PERIDOTITE

KEYS: Minerals easily seen with unaided eye. Minerals mutually intergrown. Dark color; heavy weight.

Acid Test: Does not fizz in acid.

Mineral Content: Olivine, pyroxene, hornblende.

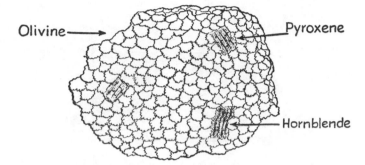

Olivine ⟶   Pyroxene

⟵ Hornblende

A dark rock resembling gabbro but heavier and containing little or no plagioclase feldspar is called peridotite. It has a comparatively high content of iron, and the color is dark green or black. The dominant mineral is olivine, and it is the French word (peridot) for this mineral that has given us this name. Pyroxene (mostly augite) and hornblende are less in quantity. Peridotite has formed under conditions of maximum temperatures and often considerable pressure. It sometimes is a valuable source of metals, notably nickel, chromium, and platinum, and in Rhode Island it contains a good deal of magnetite. The most significant mineral of any to be found in it is diamond. The diamond-bearing variety—the only proved mother rock of this gem—was named kimberlite after the South African city which is the center of the industry. The same occurrence of diamond in peridotite is known in Pike County, Ark., and in India. Other bodies of peridotite, but without diamonds, are distributed throughout the world. Tremendous volumes are present in New Caledonia and Cuba. Peridotite weathers readily to serpentine, with which asbestos may be associated.

METEORITE

Black or brown crust

Sharp metal

"Thumb prints"

Although so rare that the average mineral collector is unlikely ever to find one, meteorites are of such vital scientific importance that the chance of your coming across a specimen and failing to recognize it should be reduced as much as possible. Only about 1,550 different meteorite "falls" have been recorded to date, though some falls are represented by many separate fragments. Each fall is different from the rest, and an expert can tell from which locality any given specimen has come. The classification of meteorites embraces three major kinds. Siderites (not to be confused with the mineral siderite), or so-called iron meteorites, are metallic, consisting of an alloy of iron, nickel, and cobalt. Aerolites, or so-called stony meteorites, resemble many ordinary heavy rocks; consisting mainly of olivine and pyroxene, they always reveal at least traces of metal. Those of an intermediate type are siderolites or ironstones, an example of which are the pallasites, showing nuggets of olivine set in a handsome meshwork of metal. The brown or black iron oxide coatings and the depressions or "thumbprints" are characteristics of meteorites.

COAL

KEYS: Minerals not easily seen with unaided eye. Coal-like appearance.

Color: Black. Acid Test: Does not fizz in acid.
Mineral Content: None.

Banded

Coal is regarded as a sedimentary rock because it is found in layers or beds. All coal once existed as growing plants which died, became partly decayed, and then were preserved by burial. The original plant life was of an amazing variety, over 3,000 different species having been identified from the age of greatest coal making. Appropriately called the Carboniferous Period, this was a time of lush vegetation, when ferns grew the size of today's trees and rushes were 90 feet tall. The first stage in the forming of coal is called peat. As further burial continues, the gases and water are forced out and the material left behind is thereby enriched in carbon. Peat thus turns to lignite or brown coal, which gives way to bituminous or soft coal, and eventually to anthracite or hard coal. As these changes proceed, the coal becomes brighter and harder, and it breaks more regularly. If coal is squeezed by pressure from the sides during the building of a mountain range, the ultimate product may be the mineral graphite. The thickest seams of coal are situated in Victoria, Australia, and the most valuable are in northeastern Pennsylvania.

OBSIDIAN

KEYS: Minerals not easily seen with unaided eye. Glassy appearance. Solid body.

Color: Black. Acid Test: Does not fizz in acid.
Mineral Content: Glass.

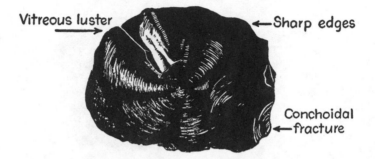

Vitreous luster ← →Sharp edges

Conchoidal ←fracture

When lava flows onto the surface of the ground and cools so quickly that separate minerals do not have time to form, the resulting natural glass is known as obsidian. Its chemical composition is such that it would have become a normal granite if it had solidified very slowly at depth. The usual jet-black color is due to the presence of tiny specks of magnetite scattered like dust so that they absorb the light. Inside, also, may be seen the beginnings of crystals which failed to grow further, and often appear in flowerlike spots. Owing to its tendency to break with sharp edges, this natural glass was a boon to the people of primitive races who used it for all sorts of implements and weapons. Obsidian Cliff in Yellowstone National Park is a noted occurrence, and Mono Lake, Calif., is another. Distinctive obsidian from certain islands in the Mediterranean is mottled in red and black and appears somewhat pitchy. True pitchstone, however, is natural glass with a higher water content than obsidian and a pitchy luster. Ultimately obsidian seems to crystallize, so that all natural glass dates from relatively modern geologic time.

176

PUMICE

KEYS: Minerals not easily seen with unaided eye. Glassy appearance. Porous body.

Color: Gray. **Acid Test:** Does not fizz in acid.

Mineral Content: Glass.

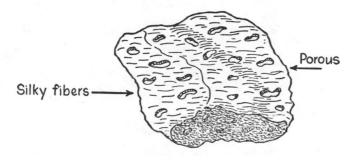

Silky fibers ⟶

Porous ⟵

Expanded by the explosion of steam as it escapes from a volcano and puffed up into a froth of glass, pumice is a foamy mass of silky glass shards. These shards may be intermixed or else drawn out in parallel strands. Its porous nature and the many isolated cells of air enable pumice to float on water for a long while, pieces of it drifting ashore on almost every seacoast before they become waterlogged. The chemical composition of pumice is like that of obsidian or granite, except as the peculiar conditions under which it was formed make a difference. Although most pumice is light-colored, some of it is brownish or occasionally red. The sharp cutting edges of the bits of glass make pumice a serviceable abrasive, used in scouring-soap and as a dental polish. The Lipari Islands, between Sicily and the mainland of Italy, have long been the leading source of commercial pumice. New Mexico, California, and Oregon produce the most American pumice. A thick bed of California pumice is mined and sliced for use as an insulating material in refrigerators. Smaller pieces are mixed with cement and plaster to give these construction materials a lighter weight.

SHALE

KEYS: Minerals not easily seen with unaided eye. Stony appearance. Can be split into layers.

Color: Gray, black. Acid Test: Does not fizz in acid.

Mineral Content: Clay.

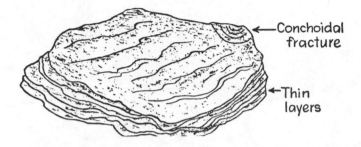

Conchoidal fracture

Thin layers

The sedimentary rock called shale consists of various clay minerals, which have ceased to be plastic and have accumulated into thin beds. The flaky grains are too tiny to be recognized at sight, but tests show them to be kaolinite and the related aluminum silicate minerals collectively known as clay. Small flakes of white mica, bits of quartz sand, and cementing limestone are commonly present, and almost any mineral can be incorporated into a shale. Lumpy inclusions called concretions are sometimes large. Shale is a soft and easily eroded rock, and it can be split with little effort. Some black shale is rich in carbon; other shale is gray or almost any color. Fuel has been produced from oil shale in Scotland for a century; the colossal reserves in western Colorado and eastern Utah are said to be the largest mineral deposit in the world except the ocean. Its weakness prevents the use of shale as a building stone, but this rock, abundant throughout the globe, has value as a mixing substance in the manufacture of cement. As shale increases in coarseness by the addition of sand, it grades into siltstone.

178

SCHIST

KEYS: Minerals not easily seen with unaided eye. Stony appearance. Can be split into layers.

Color: Variable. Acid Test: Does not fizz in acid.

Mineral Content: Variable.

Fine banding ⟶

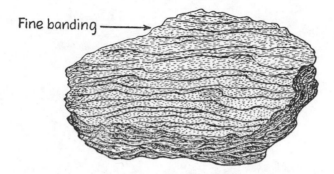

Schist is a closely layered metamorphic rock. Its name comes from the Greek word meaning "to divide," because of the ease with which it can be split between the layers. These layers are narrower than those of gneiss, but the two kinds of rock grade into each other, and no definite line can be drawn between them. As a rule, adjacent layers in a schist consist of the same minerals, and so schist is much more uniform in appearance and composition than gneiss. To this fact it owes much of its ability to separate by splitting. Unlike gneiss, schist is not so likely to contain feldspar as a significant mineral. Mica, instead, is extremely common; mica schist, composed of quartz associated with abundant flakes of black biotite or silvery muscovite, is the most widespread variety of schist and separates the most readily. Hornblende schist is another important rock, and there are other kinds of schist marked by red garnet, green chlorite, shiny-gray graphite, or white talc. These often make colorful specimens. As the layers of schist become still narrower, the rock grades into phyllite and then into slate.

SLATE

KEYS: Minerals not easily seen with unaided eye. Stony appearance. Can be split into layers.

Color: Gray. Acid Test: Does not fizz in acid.

Mineral Content: Clay.

Sharp edges ⟶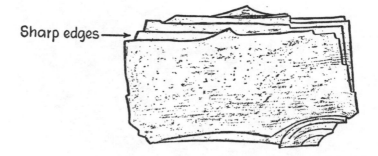

Intense pressure acting on beds of shale changes them to slate, a metamorphic rock. As a result, a smooth cleavage is developed at an angle to the original bedding and straight across the direction of pressure. The individual grains, like those in shale, are too small to be visibly recognized without magnification. Although the normal color of slate is dark gray, inclining toward black, varieties are known which are red, green, purple, or brown. Some slate contains conspicuous crystals of pyrite, well-shaped and attractive against their dark background. Another kind of slate with inclusions is knotted slate, having coarse crystals of silicate minerals scattered through it; this slate indicates the nearness of an igneous rock and a possible ore deposit. As might be expected, slate occurs in mountainous regions where the required pressure was developed in past ages. Commercial production in the United States, for blackboards and roofing purposes, is carried on mostly in Pennsylvania and Vermont. Broad, thin sheets of extraordinary size are quarried at Pen Argyl, Pa. Otherwise useful deposits may be too far from adequate markets.

LIMESTONE

KEYS: Minerals not easily seen with unaided eye. Stony appearance. Cannot be split into layers. Fizzes in acid. Color: White. **Mineral Content:** Calcite, dolomite.

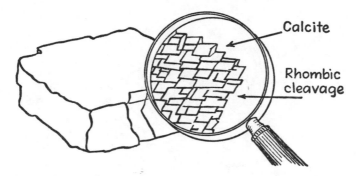

Calcite

Rhombic cleavage

Limestone is a sedimentary rock composed solely of one mineral, calcite. It is generally white or gray, except when impurities cause a darkening. Limestone can be formed through the life processes of a wide range of organisms, from one-celled plants, such as algae, to specialized animals, such as corals. These extract calcium carbonate from the water and use it to build their skeletons and shells. Limestone also can be deposited inorganically, by strictly chemical means. There are many different kinds of limestone. A well-known one is chalk, which seems to be a fine powder until seen under a microscope, when it proves to be made up mostly of the remains of tiny, single-celled animals called foraminifers. Coquina is limestone composed of an accumulation of loosely packed shells, cemented together firmly enough so that it is used in Florida as a building stone. Travertine is porous limestone deposited by hot springs. So-called Mexican onyx, familiar in pen stands and clock cases, is limestone marked by swirling patterns in attractive colors. Most cave stalactites and stalagmites are built of limestone.

MARBLE

KEYS: Minerals not easily seen with unaided eye. Stony
appearance. Cannot be split into layers. Fizzes in acid.
Color: White, gray. Mineral Content: Calcite.

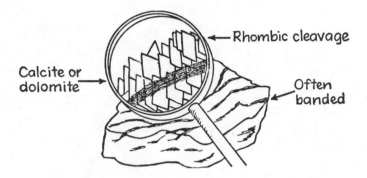

When either limestone or dolomite is drastically changed
by heat, pressure, and water, the new metamorphic rock
is termed marble. The agents that produce this trans-
formation enable the grains of calcite or dolomite to
grow larger and to give the surface a livelier sparkle than
before. Any impurities that were present in the original
rock or that were introduced during the change tend to
be segregated into knots or spread out in wavy streaks,
producing the varicolored "marbling" that is so appealing a feature of ornamental marble. North Africa produces superb examples of such stone. Snow-white marble,
such as the famous stone from Carrara, Italy, is favored
for statuary purposes. Similar Pentelic marble from
Greece was sculptured into the priceless creations that
are so enduring a heritage of Hellenic civilization. The
Yule marble from Colorado, of which a single block
weighing 56 tons was required for the Tomb of the Unknown Soldier, is equal to any from the Mediterranean
region. Architectural marble is characterized by its uniform color. Vermont, Tennessee, and Georgia are states
quarrying important amounts of marble.

SANDSTONE

KEYS: Minerals not easily seen with unaided eye. Stony appearance. Cannot be split into layers. Does not fizz in acid.

Color: White, brown. Mineral Content: Quartz.

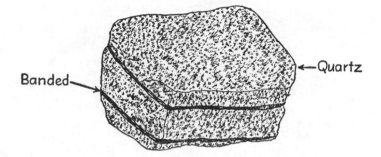

An accumulation of grains of quartz sand, cemented together more or less firmly to become rock, is called sandstone. As sandstone becomes coarse, it grades into conglomerate; as it becomes finer, it grades into siltstone. Some sandstone, such as the Potsdam sandstone of Wisconsin, is remarkably pure, consisting of little except quartz. Other specimens contain feldspar in increasing proportions, flakes of mica, and small grains of heavy minerals typical of placer deposits. The color of sandstone depends largely on the nature of the cement; iron oxide gives the red, yellow, and brown shades. A limy cement will fizz in acid but not the mineral grains. The shape of the individual particles likewise varies from perfectly round to sharply angular. Sandstone that splits readily into even slabs is known as flagstone. Brownstone, once the most fashionable building stone in Philadelphia, New York, and other Northeastern cities, is a sandstone containing considerable reddish feldspar. The most extraordinary kind of sandstone, called itacolumite, is actually flexible; a slab of it from North Carolina or Brazil will bend under its own weight.

QUARTZITE

KEYS: Minerals not easily seen with unaided eye. Stony appearance. Cannot be split into layers. Does not fizz in acid.

Color: White. Mineral Content: Quartz.

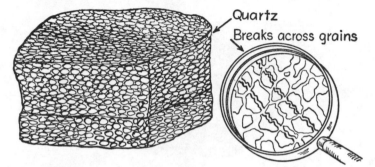

Quartz

Breaks across grains

When subjected to pressure or heat, sandstone is changed to the metamorphic rock know as quartzite. This name, which indicates that quartz is practically the sole mineral present, is also applied by many geologists to ordinary sandstone which has merely been cemented together more tightly than usual. A true quartzite, however—the toughest of all rocks—will break across the sand grains instead of having to break around them, because the former cementing material in the original sandstone has become as hard as the grains themselves. During the processes of change, moreover, some of the previous cement is likely to be recrystallized into small quantities of a number of new minerals, such as garnet, epidote, graphite, and muscovite mica. These may give color to an otherwise white rock. Quartzite used industrially as a heat-resisting material is called ganister. Burrstone is a porous variety of quartzite used for millstones. The Quartzite Range in British Columbia is named from its exposures of very old quartzite. The Baraboo quartzite is a handsomely crystalline rock, often deep-red in color, well exposed in Wisconsin.

FELSITE

KEYS: Minerals not easily seen with unaided eye. Stony appearance. Cannot be split into layers. Does not fizz in acid.

Color: White, gray. Mineral Content: Feldspar.

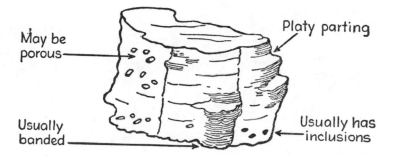

May be porous

Platy parting

Usually banded

Usually has inclusions

Light-colored igneous rocks that are so fine-grained that the constituent minerals can scarcely be recognized without a microscope are grouped together under the name felsite. They may be of any color but are light in tone, as contrasted with basalt, which is dark. The difference is basically due to the kinds of minerals that are present, and this is impossible to determine with the unaided eye. With a hand lens, however, perhaps the translucent edges of the feldspar, which is the chief mineral in felsite, can be observed even in some of the darker-looking specimens. Felsite originates mainly in lava flows and is abundant on a world-wide scale. One of the most important types is rhyolite, which makes up a large part of Yellowstone National Park. Phonolite contains the gold ores at Cripple Creek, Colo. It emits a ringing sound when struck; hence its name. Trachyte is prominent along the Rhine River, in central France, and in the Black Hills of South Dakota. Andesite is represented by a series of high volcanic cones stretching from Mount Rainier, Wash., through Mexico and Central America, all the way to the far tip of the Andes.

BASALT

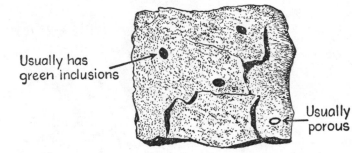

Usually has green inclusions

Usually porous

A heavy dark rock with a fine-grained texture, basalt is the most abundant of the rocks which have cooled from sheets or flows of lava. The gas escaping from the molten matter as it rises to the surface of the earth leaves oval cavities, which later are often lined or completely filled with minerals. The chief mineral that is readily visible against the dark background is olivine, which usually appears as green particles the size of buckshot. Of all the various kinds of rock, basalt is the one most likely to be divided by columnar jointing, which produces long upright pillars. The scenic Giant's Causeway on the north coast of Ireland is perhaps the most impressive example. Basalt occurs in small bodies as well, but the largest ones are of incredible extent. The Hawaiian Islands are built almost entirely of basalt, which erupted from numerous vents. The Columbia River region in the Northwestern section of the United States was blanketed by basalt, to create much of its present landscape. The Deccan region of India contains nearly one-quarter million square miles of basalt, which was piled as much as 10,000 feet thick.

Magazines for the Collector

The following magazines are national publications devoted to mineral and rock collecting and related hobbies. In addition there are various smaller but good periodicals of regional circulation and numerous specialized professional journals which may be consulted in public or college libraries.

Gems and Minerals, edited by Don MacLachlan, has short illustrated articles on the various phases of mineral collecting. It is published monthly at Mentone, Calif.; the subscription price is $3.00 per year.

The Mineralogist, edited by Don MacLachlan, deals especially with the collecting of mineral specimens. It is published bimonthly at Mentone, Calif.; the subscription price is $2.00 per year.

Rocks and Minerals, edited since 1926 by Peter Zodac, covers in popular language the entire field of minerals and rocks. It is published bimonthly at Box 29, Peekskill, N. Y.; the subscription price is $3.00 per year.

Earth Science, edited by Dr. Ben H. Wilson, includes worthwhile articles on minerals, rocks, and popular geology. It is published bimonthly at Box 1357, Chicago 90, Ill.; the subscription price is $2.50 per year.

The Lapidary Journal, edited by Hugh Leiper, specializes in the collecting and cutting of gems and ornamental stones. It is published monthly at P.O. Box 2369, San Diego 12, Calif.; the subscription price is $4.50 per year.

The Desert Magazine, edited by Eugene L. Conrotto, features articles on mineral localities in Southwestern United States, illustrated with helpful maps. It is published monthly at Palm Desert, Calif.; the subscription price is $4.50 per year.

Books for the Collector

The following books are especially recommended for further reading and reference. The classifications and brief descriptive notes are intended to aid the purchaser.

INTRODUCTORY
Getting Acquainted with Minerals by George L. English, revised by David E. Jensen, published by McGraw-Hill Book Company, Inc., New York (2d ed., 1958). An attractive book to stimulate a beginner.

TEXTBOOK
Minerals and How to Study Them by Edward Salisbury Dana, revised by Cornelius S. Hurlbut, Jr., published by John Wiley & Sons, Inc., New York (3d ed., 1949). Well illustrated.

REFERENCE
1001 Questions Answered About the Mineral Kingdom by Richard M. Pearl, published by Dodd, Mead & Company, New York (1959). Deals with various aspects of minerals and rocks.

GEMS
Popular Gemology by Richard M. Pearl, published by Sage Books, Denver (2d ed., 1958). A scientifically accurate, finely illustrated book on gems, clearly written in layman's language.

PROSPECTING
Successful Prospecting and Mineral Collecting by Richard M. Pearl, published by McGraw-Hill Book Company, Inc., New York (1961). Illustrated book on both phases of mineral collecting.

LOCALITIES
American Gem Trails by Richard M. Pearl, published by McGraw-Hill Book Company, Inc., New York (1962). Brief mention of many collecting localities throughout the United States.

Colorado Gem Trails and Mineral Guide by Richard M. Pearl, published by Sage Books, Denver (1958). A detailed guide with many maps.

Numerous other regional locality guides are available.

Index